A Manual for the Use of Students in Egyptology

Edward Yorke McCauley

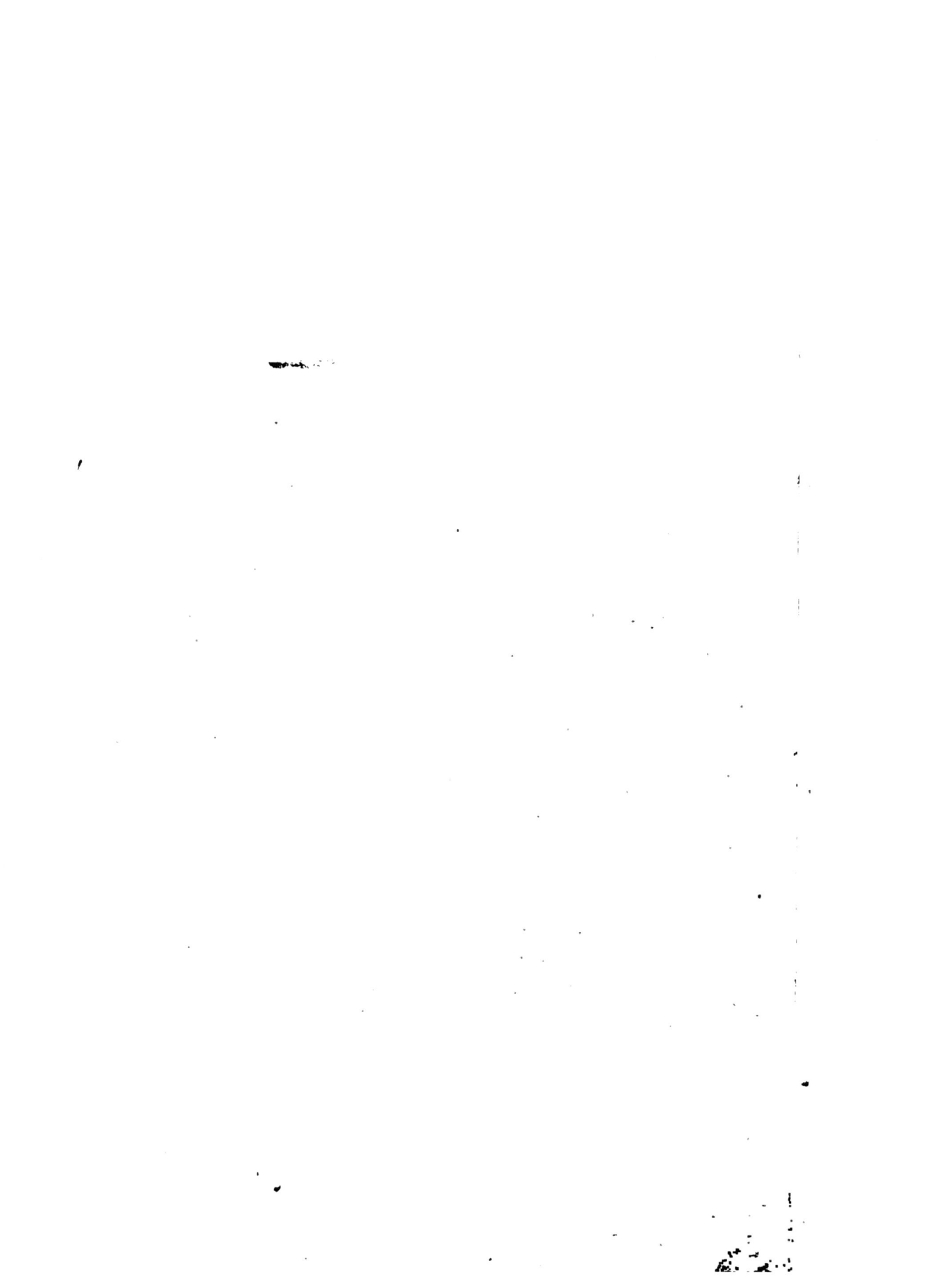

OMISSION FROM THE INDEX OF VOL. XIX.

Communication,

PROCEEDINGS

OF THE

AMERICAN PHILOSOPHICAL SOCIETY,

HELD AT PHILADELPHIA, FOR PROMOTING USEFUL KNOWLEDGE.

VOL. XX.	1881.	No. 110.

TABLE OF CONTENTS.

C

4.

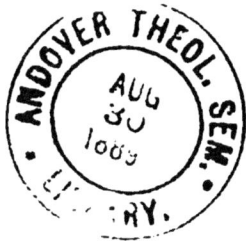

A Manual for the Use of Students in Egyptology. By Edward Yorke McCauley, U. S. N.

(Read before the American Philosophical Society, July, 1881.)

Preface

———

In the following "Manual", compiled from the authorities within my reach, will be found much information which, after the first elementary knowledge has been acquired, is essential to progress in the study of Egyptology

No attempt, that I am aware of, has been hitherto made to bring together within the compass of one volume, and in its present fullness, the results of the learned labors of Egyptologists eminent in this department. To obtain these results, requires an extensive and expensive library and many days of patient labor and research.

In a department of knowledge where our metes and bounds are constantly widening it would be presumptuous to assume that the lists, I have given, of Gods, of symbols, Names of Countries &c comprise all that are known or that may be found in hieroglyphic texts: Those, in all cases are given which are of daily occurrence.

The student will observe, in my List of Ideographs, that, not content with giving the main idea only, of which any single example is the exponent, as is generally the case, I give a list of the terms which start from the Parent ideograph; By this amplification, which is far from complete, a conception may be formed of the general value or tenor of the ideograph.

It must be borne in mind that I have not undertaken to give any general outline of Hieroglyphics during the thousands of years covered by Egyptian history, in which, what may have been correct at one period may be changed at another; Wherefore, although errors undoubtedly occur in the following pages (*Errare est, &c*), haste in imputing them is to be deprecated.

It gives me pleasure to acknowledge the constant aid and encouragement which I have received from I. P. Lesley L. L. D. and also the untiring courtesy extended to me by Mr. Lloyd P. Smith and his assistant Mr. B. Samuel at the Ridgeway Library.

Philadelphia   Edward Yorke McCauley

1st Nov: 1881.   U. S. Navy

ALPHABET.

	sound	object		sound	object		sound	object		sound	object		sound	object
	a	reed top		ab	hide		at	thread		ab			hat	plough
	apt			a	arm		ap			ba			her	
	xu			at			aak	moon		ba	bull		heg	crook
	a	paddle		ax xu			a			ba	ram		hn	
	ahse	goose		ax abh			an			b	hawk		hn	
	am ham			at kt			dat			b	heron		ha	
	ab	column		au ab ub			dsh	lizard		b	basket fruit		ha ten ui ha	
	ab			ub			ap			fi	worm		
	ai	come		ab			ir ar			f			hu	
	ab ub			ab			a			f Ga la			hu	lusk
	am	tree		ab.			an			hu			han	vase
	am	cross		ab			a			hi			hut	onion
	ap lep	head		a			amx			ha			htp	table
	ap	horns		aa yaa	calf		a			ha			her	
	ap			au yau			a			ha			han	vase
	as	noble		a	eagle		ahn hem			ha			ht	
	as			ad			a			ha			ht	
	as			hab ab	bee		bu	leg furnace		ha			hut	
	as a	papyrus		dry an			ba			hm			ka	
	hu	post		un dr at lem	strip of stuff		ba xax			hm			kes	
	an	mast		an			du xa			hm			hp	
	an			un	hide		bgr	pyramid		hm			her	

ALPHABET.

ALPHABET.

p
pox paddle
pst bow
hr pat sky
paut eye-ball
poh
poh
pu
pot
paut
roti
ras balance post
resh plant
ar
r
r lotus leaf
r knife
r
sa quiver top
sa
su
sat
setp
sen tat
su chair back
tes bolt
se
su meadow
su shoot
seat seb
sud
s
seb ring
su egg
sem spade
sen shen
s shes
sper lip
serk
sut cow car
sut
se goose
sat
sen lion-ess
sep shep
s sh
ser
ser
ser
sn shen
sn shen
sex
seb flute
sa woof
sep
sa woof
sap
sep
sap
sak
sau
sat
sat
s
tu club
ta land
ta
ta
ta
ta
tu side
tut hand
ti thread
t mul-ler
tab dress
shem
tom
tob
tom sledge
tor
lor
ler
tos
tat
ga
ta
losr
la
ga
ta
ler
ta boat
tat pallette
lat
lat give
tu
t shoot
t
tos chis-el
t
t bread basket
lu
lu
t boat net

ALPHABET.

	tau		ut		ẋem		
	tāp	adze	uk		ẋ	fig	
	tōr	muzzle	sh	pool	ẋa	stool	
	tān		shen	ring	ẋ		
	tāh		shelu				
	tōt	finger	shep				
	ud	pullet	sha	sun rising			
	ur	sparrow	sha	"			
	u	thread	shu	feather			
	ua	lotus	sha	field			
	nat	sceptre	shent	Vases			
	ua		shent	"			
	uah		shes	sled			
	ua		ẋa	mace			
	uah		ẋa	sturgeon			
	uah		ẋa	lotus leaf			
	usef		ẋaf				
	ut		ẋi	seire			
	usr		ẋem				
	ur		ẋen				
	nat		ẋẋr				
			ẋa				

Index of determinatives, &c.

Man fallen 11	Papyrus roll 332,340	Road 55	Stone 74	Water clock
" sitting 13	Pectoral 297	Roll 332,340	String of beads 299	Water, 6 425
" squatting 10	Pellet 193	Sail 77	Sun 2	Weight 327
" standing 12	Pelvis 162	Sandal 306	Sword 91	Wells 241
" walking 10	Pen, reed 328	Saw 98	Table 400	Whetstone
Man's head 16	Persea tree 46	Scales 142	Tablet 268	Whip, 344 392
Manger 372	Phallus 28	Scarab 14	Tadpole 32	Wigs 285
Mantis 32	Pile of bricks 72	Sceptre 330	Temple 55	Wings 42
Marsh 125	Plants 47	Scorpion 32	Testes 31	Woman
Mason's? 67	Plough 127	Seal 104	Throne 32	squatting 10
Measure 119,4?	Plume 302	Seat 254	Tiger-skin 167	World 157
Metal 108	Polisher 333	Shekel 191	Tomb door 59	Worm 32
Mirror 114	Pod 48	Shoe tie 309	Tooth 19	Zero 188
Moon 3	Pool 125	Shrine 265	Tortoise 32	
Mouth 158	Posts of balance 141	Shutter 366	Tower 56	
Muller 407	Pot on legs 195	Sickle 128	Tree 45	
Mummy 11	Props 315	Signet 104	Truss of hay 185	
" hawk 40	Pygmy 12	Sistrum 310	Tusk 18	
Neb 369	Pylon 253	Skin 32	Twig 52	
Net 344	Pyramid 376, 429	Sled 201	Vase 9	
Numerals 181	" & star 219	Sling 431	Utensils 96,411	
Obelisk 257	Quiver 378	Sofa 262	Vines 48	
Onion 225	Reed pen 328	Soles 221	Vulture 40	
Ordinals 188	" top 239	Spindle 339	" head 41	
Ornament 419	" on legs 194	Square 67	Wall 56	
Packet 107	Reeling 337	Standard 130	" fort 69	
Palanquin 263	Rib 403	Star 4	Wasp 32	
Palm 48	Rigging 78	Steps 58		
Palette 325	Ring 100,102	Stibium 355		
Panegyries 75		Stick 53		

INDEX OF NONDESCRIPTS.

INDEX OF NONDESCRIPTS.

INDEX OF NONDESCRIPTS.

IDEOGRAPHS AND DETERMINATIVES.

⊓	pet / agu / ayt / Aqi / Xe / har / heri	sky, heaven / suspend / ceiling / elevation / over, above / chief	1	⚘ / ⚲ / ⚮	ali / het / ubn / mau / ui / auti / hai / ani / Xu	sunbeam / sun's rays / daylight / illuminate / gleam / brilliancy / bright, clear / light / a beam / light
⌐	Kar	half heaven / course of the sun		✪	suau / "	abode of stars / sub division of celestial world / gate
⪢	Latu / haiu / shema / ubkth / stahn / akap	twist, distort / obstruct / storm, rain		🪶	hut / .	celestial sun / good demon
⊞	xena / apkti	to turn away / loss, injury		⬯		
⋕	tahen			⏝ / ⬭ / ⊙	aya / sbyx / ayut	horizon / solar dwelling / solar mountains
⊤	axx / uya / xarh / axrh / KH	night / darkness / night / obscurity		⬭ / ◌	api / ka	
⊤	ashru	darkness		⌒	d / aah / ait / ina / Xat	lunar time / moon / moon / month / fortnight / phase, eclipse	J
⊙	Ra / ain / kru / sht / ubys / pst / renpa / han / sef / Kar / Koh / hev	the sun / solar disk / day / to light / to shine / to gleam / year / day / yesterday / sunset / night / festival	2	✦	sba / hau / seb / abt / Zha / kru / Nap / apt / at	star / adore, gate, soul / month / fortnight / hour / hour / constellation / swan / star	4
				✦	annut	the Gods

IDEOGRAPHS AND DETERMINATIVES.

	set	a hill	5		srut (rut)	dig, engrave, plant, grow, germinate
	selu	foreign lands			akana	goblet
	meru	isle			arp	wine
	mer mu mau ab sa, su shr slafu	sea, waters water " thirst, pure drink " refine, melt	6		hek ham buka iua aft Arku mrku hanni anhu	drink vase conserve, balsam to wash pitch, cedar-oil to anoint to wax tribute
	am	amid - of Egypt	7		art ashr ashbu ruxa aʃm rex	milk inflame consume brazier extinguish brazier
	apt	ideograph of verbs in general, of every action, as getting up and shutting the door, judging &c specially arrived to judge			tat mrh kati Haknu ausa adr slti	oil wax extract, essence drug perfume ambergris perfume
	anx xetama s'anx	crux ansata life, smut to nourish, food, subsist.	8		tat kati mrhu	oil essence, extract wax
		anx uta Snab, an invocation Life! health! strength			kes amurt nem kam	jug a liquid a liquid
	ef neser	fire, flame, steam flame	9		kan	Majesty, purity
	ker neser	the house of flame, the Eastern horizon.			Kabh heh	liquids, refreshments to vex, enrage
	aʃm bakau	extinguished something eaten				
	kan kati krt ax shaka mat	peaceful heart, intention peaceful lovely, gay granite			Nka	liquids, refreshments
	snf ByY muau xt xp xu	blood y, water				

IDEOGRAPHS AND DETERMINATIVES.

	nu	jar, ampulla 9 cont:			of action of mind and mouth
	han	vase		a	I, me, my, myself
	tes	a liquid, liquid meas-		fet	to disquiet, to fail
		ure		anan	to murmur, to be, being
	nehat	vapor		hekna	to discourse, to supplicate
	pes	to cook		hek	to charm, magic
				amlu	caste, rank
	nemmut	a liquid		ah	move
				aftu	acquaint, judge
	xum	God Chumnis		apt	suck
				aau	extend
	kesu	praise		ab	oppose
				annu	howl
	shentt	dwelling in, living in		ash	cry, plaint
				ax	ruler
				abh	wish, favor
				hanp	to spy, a deserter
				ha	hailer
	atn	a substance		ham hamt-	to roar
	kab	a liquid		hutr	to order
		tesh		ker	silence
	nams	a liquid		kar	fault
				mat	reverence
	peka	a gap		mahaut-	homage, obey
	stm	stibium			living persons
	hemka	jasper			
	asu	servant, satellite 10		ari	to guard, to keep,
	amnu	captain			companion
	at	labour, follower, compan.		hems	of peaceful action
	ayu	spirit, light			to sit
	asi	noble		tka	to prostrate
				hft	to squat
				kha	miserable
				besht	to revolt, to rebel
				nini	quiet, rest
				at	labor, produce.
				suau	to adore
				sbau	to glorify
	mallu	troops, mercenaries		mx	archer soldier
	anti	men of the gate		meh	
	amuth	a title		xab	of dance
	apa	ancestor		abu	to sport
	as	noble, great-		heknu	to dance
	as	statue		ha	to welcome, to address
	apu	ton maker		ux	Oh! Hail
	a	I, me, my, myself			to turn
				kat	to build, to labor
				uau	variant of a star

IDEOGRAPHS AND DETERMINATIVES.

	xabu	ellipid 10 cent.		nat	to knead
	sbau xeft	a convict: impious enemy		beshtu Uhu	weak prisoner
	nub netKi.	to gild to work in gold.		beshtu Uhu	weak prisoner
	ha aau	to rejoice to adore, praise, exalt		nesh tut apa bes	statue " ancestor noble to please, acquaint, fill
	hanna Tehh	suppliant rejoice		Aan hanti han han	turn back returner command
	ha em	heh, a trillion years illimitably, for ever		pati rexitu tasu mehtu	people intelligent beings people of S. Egypt " " N. "
	hes	to sing			
	amn	to hide		ax axu	spirit manes
	sxai	a scribe		mahahuit akiu amam mer ait	courtiers' family inferior beholders superintendants of fire
	fa	to bear, to carry		set Stu Bar satu mha	Typhon " Baal Sadok al ass
	Shur or sur	to drink			of names of females and Goddesses.
	ab an	pure, priest scribe "			
	Kebeh	libation			
					of parturition
	Stem	a judge		men men a ver xem	to bring up to suckle, a wet nurse to dandle " " to put to sleep
	neham	to save		stesi ap	to drag along supine "

IDEOGRAPHS AND DETERMINATIVES.

		over throw
	Xtb	overthrow
	Xr.ehr	smite
	sfx	lay waste
	hefu	growl
	mehbi	to humble
	bukli	malefactor
	het mi	obscure
	reital	rebel, culpable
	Xeft	enemies, the impious
	seb	profane
	Xebli	transformation / sha accuse
	lut	image / aru ceremony
	Karo	mummy / Ka a form
		of embalmming
	aut	matter
	Xat	a body
	Kars	embalm
	hes	obedient
	ab	form, type, image
	ox	dead, spirit, type
	Xtb	tumble
	pet	heavens, the sky
	nebkt	to wash gold / to swim
	hi / ufa / Xem / Kat	strike of construction 12 / chastise / build, construct "
	hi / ufa / ten / amenfiu / betsh / betnu	strike / chastise / bruise / hide / lazy, slow, injure / malefactor
	aau / eKa	joy, acclamation / exalt, praise
	Ka	bearer, wearer (of dia-dem)
	Ka	to bear, support, extend / Ra who extends the heavens.

	nini / Kebeh	sprinkle / libation
	sems	older, prince, prefer-red, adopted
	Hes	to beg, beseech
	uxe	create, mould
	sbau	praise, glorification
	Xet / ba	invert / topsy-turvy
	nnim	pygmy
	amn / hak	conceal, envellop / captive
	heter-han	high priest
	annu	to look back
	satem / ab / ash	listen / hear, listen / cry, plaint
	tenh	to blind, of Asiatic captive

IDEOGRAPHS AND DETERMINATIVES.

		Negro captive /2		χa	to measure corn
		chief		hes teχen	to sing to play the harp
	maan	cattle guard			
	χiχi	to whip		lll χeteb	to subdue " "
	ta Seb	to offer sacrifice " drink			
	maan	cattle feeder, driver		tut	statue
	ma			bu Kes	of metal (with ☒☒ as töne) subdue, overcome, vanquish
	ash pherr	cry, plaint			
	aba	to play a game			
	Kebeh	libation		herri	Quadrigga
	neham	rejoice		tut	a statue
	mert bak aχ aχela anan fu	powerful servant mow babble, want hoe strike		shr	to terrify
	set	spill. pourout			
	uah Kebeh	pour out, to feed libation		hur	elder
	ain	to beat, to pound			

IDEOGRAPHS AND DETERMINATIVES.

	sla	prisoner, convey		ahi ta	upon earth	16.
				ahi ru	palate, edge of life	
				ahi ro	dedication	
				ahi	forthwith	
	ur	elder		her	on, upon, face	
	ahr or ahii	assistant priestess		ru	mouth	
	hems	to sit		slem	stibium	17
				an	appear, show.	
	xen	baby of youth				
	ru	nursling				
	xer	child				
	xart	offspring		ka	to spy	hestourz stare
	mpa	to grow		an	adorn	ava, to pierce
	ohru	to nurse		nhas	raise up	atn nu sleep
	mahar	youth, hero, Soldier		res	suspend	agt, splendor
	se	son		xer	content	
	xrut	child				
	efi					
	an	move				
	aht	acquaint, judge		ari	eye	
	amten	caste, rank		nimi	weep	
				axn	shut the eye, wink	
	atn	to build, form, create		atnt	build, form, sleep	
	abn	to build, form, fashion		ar	author	
				artu	works	
				ar	produced by _	
				ar	to make	
	xhr	scarab	14	ab	passage	
	xprta	earth, world		ab	frontage	
	afi	fly		armta	to see	
	ment	bier of embalming	15	nimi	tears	
				rem	weep	
	menat	repose; death		akb	lament	
	nent	bier, couch				
	xat	a body		an	precinct	
	etr	to lay out				
	kar	to embalm				
	menau	sleep, death		an	appear, show	
	afu	head of the head	16	ath	tooth	18.
	ap	equal		ta	pay	
	apitani	forehead		kaka	to chew, gobble up	
	ha	face		hu	food	
	tatu	head				

IDEOGRAPHS AND DETERMINATIVES.

✎		of land, working the earth and of angular objects.	⟋	ser	brush, reserve, private, effect, oblique, sacred, involved.
	ta	tooth, earth, to swallow			
	hiu	means, taste, perception			
	henbt	fountain			
	apt	corner		ser	distribute, chosen, holy. venerable
	apt	horizon 19			
	ab	clear			(all of this type seem to have the same value)
	abehu	tooth			
	nu	cultivate			
△	tat	give, send 20	⟋	ser	arrange
⌐	Kab	arm		meha	leave
⟺	Kabi	a pair of arms		xu	rule
{}	Kan heft anh aka apt	breast unite embrace divide rib			of painting
{|}	tani habtu	to encircle to hold together		Kar Kat	to fight to contend, to kill
{|}			⌐	ma	directly, presently
←	akhut ar aau auaa aa aua aufu aut auau au auai	prepare of power light, honor, suspend reproach steal, take knit captain chastise " " length kidnap, gainsay, catch	▼▼	mna snkau or shkau	to nurse 21 } to suckle
		of peaceful action	⊓		labyrinth 22
⌐	Kuhu	shoulder		Kar Ker uuh Kru	to rob, entrap, hasten secret, harass, ravish to hold, possess 24 to entice garrison
⟋	Xu, xu	to rule, protect, screen a fan	⎰⎰	Sati apu	the feet guide, police
⟋	xu	to rule	⎰	en ret xent uar bu ar around sutan hama apt peter en ta	knee foot approach leg " acre " lie down terrible, roar guide, lead, propose to kneel
⟋	Xu	to rule			

IDEOGRAPHS AND DETERMINATIVES.

		Symbol	Transliteration	Meaning	No.
skau tha maken bennu sati	sacrifice drunk, deprive slaughter no, not anihilate	24	sam sam	horse	
heh ait	of motion wander, search asleep, apace		aua ka aka	bull of cattle fat	
sna yesef hem annu	turn away slip, not go slay rise, hold		ah aua maht kau	cow white antelope cow	
masi (ameni)	brought, conduct, "les apports", cargo, merchandise		abhem aua hnhr hueu ab	calf steer calf thirst	
art	of parts of the body rump	25	salf ba	thigh cow	
lash	fleshy part	26	sha fenti besn rex yenn sen	nostril of breathing nose breathe joy sleep breathe of dwelling	
shaa aau	to be born, flesh shoulder	27	reru yau apha	boar sow hog	
ha ka ua hau embah harmata	husband of males bull ass husband before, in presence foreskin	28	ab kamer apt bes tab xener ab hati leher	elephant of quadrupeds camel Thebes, hippopotamius askin sandal casque apiece of linen, pied bellows leather	
sa han	of the body side binds, strands	29	ba	goat, soul	
ab abu	a game of Chess Numidian goat	30	serr	Egyptian sheep	
asui	testes	31		wild goat	
htar besm rmi	horse mare cattle	32	kax xahei	gazelle "	
			ar at	antellope "	
			sehak ska sahu	ancestor to collect a crowd race, family, ancestors	

IDEOGRAPHS AND DETERMINATIVES.

	set na	an ass	82 cont⁺		ab	elephant
	uhar	dog			hunt	a wolf
					sa	a fox, a son, an order of priests
	xau	cat				rhinoceros
	teshi	tom-cat			apt	hippopotamus
	maaft	lynx				giraffe
		rat				gryphon
		gerboa rat				sphynx
	aani	ape priest			emsuh atu ayem ati	crocodile " extinguish lay out
	hati	worship			sau	connection, beam
	kant	rage			anx an	hare being, existence
					apsh	tortoise
					hek	frog, numerous
	seb ansh	jackal, crafty, cunning. magus wolf, dog			ashu	tadpole, many. numerous, million
						innumerable, more than 10.000
					fnti	blind worm
	maau	lion			aqu or ashu	lizard, numerous, to supply, to give breath to.
	sen	lioness, turn back			serk	scorpion

IDEOGRAPHS AND DETERMINATIVES.

	hem or senhem	Locust or grasshopper	32 cont.
	het / xep / hab	bee / wasp / King of W. & L. Egypt	
	af	fly	
		mantis	
	ehft / tentn / xeft / xex / bet / ahit / am	ram, to fashion 33 / to rise up, pride, revolt / demon, liar / the throat / the gullet / the windpipe / to eat	
	ela	to conduct	
	ehft / tenth / xeft / seshi / Nefau	ram, to fashion / to rise up, pride / demon, liar / place in writing / desolation	
	ah	flesh	
		thirsty	
		dorcas goat	
	pehti / apehpeh	vigilant / gigantic	
	Nenbet	subject, servant	
	Kfu / tentn / xept / Nefa / emNefau	disturb, hunt 35 / rise up, pride / thigh / seize / on the contrary	

	sotem / atn	(a sort ear) listen, heard / penetrate, regulate	36
	besiu / tehan	pass / elevate, promote	37
	palu	mortals	
	mut	die	
	Kaf / enKaf / tah tah / ta or tam / ant	carry / bear off / steal / claw	
	Xpsh	a thigh . of fame	38
		a span measure	39
	repat	lord	40
	se / Xpr / sinn / xenn / Kai	son, daughter / scarab / destroy / aleph / title	
	tai	half	
	bau	souls	
	ta	seize grasp	
	ru / terp / sent	duck / kind of duck / to prove, fear, terror, timid	
	hat	beginning	
	abhubak / bah / abahu	bird on corn heap inundation, foewill, harvest / full, inundate, supply / to gorge	
	pat / tennu / ser / maten / Nem	to fly / to move / kind of goose / facilitate / cereals, produce	

IDEOGRAPHS AND DETERMINATIVES.

	ur	of evil		akam	wrapped up
	ulā	sparrow 40 cont.		asham	eagle or falcon
	an	little			
	ak	deficient, vain		ast	to frighten, to protect
	ban	starve, hurt			
	bekau	unclean		tasher	an adjutant, red
	bek	waste, void, cease			
	but	cease, depress		hem	to find of seeking
	fennu	abominable			
	fekti	filthy, dirty			
	Kar	evade			
	han	starve, famish			
	han nu	envy, malice			
	hesm	conspire			
	haiu	suffocate		ba	soul.
	hat	destroy			
	het	fear		sex	nest, waterplace, to fill
	hut	oppress			
	xen	afflict		seshi	nest, marsh, nets
	xefen	little			
	her	false		rex	pure, soul, dream
	emsah	mislay			
	mas	halt		rex	pure, soul, dream
	makau	officer's family			
	mayam	desolate		rex	pure, spirit, wise
	anbu	thorn		rexilu	intelligent, reasoning beings
	xen	agitate, diligent,		ut	belonging to
	kam	tell, fearful		neh	drag, agitate
	tennu	to move			
	rex	pure, spirit, dream			
	ba	soul, spirit			
	an	be		anti	the perfume of Anti
	aba	pass through, opposite			
	am	give		ha	predecessor
	amma	find			
	shem	strangle, bind		ba	soul.
	tam	wicked, match			
	hma	to fish			
	Mut	mother			
	atmu	food of the dead			
	tefau	teal or small duck			
	tef	fragrance			
	sek	to be idle (snared bird)			
	ba	" " "			
	s'baat	" " "			
	setet	to tremble			

IDEOGRAPHS AND DETERMINATIVES.

	nu, nan	jar, ampulla, vase	9 cont		a, fet	of action of mind and mouth / I, me, my, myself / to disquiet, to fail
	tes	a liquid, liquid measure			anan	to murmur, to be, being
	nehat, pes	vapor / to cook			hekna	to discourse, to supplicate
	nemmut	a liquid			hek	to charm, magic
	xum	God Chumnis			amtu	caste, rank
	hosu	praise			ap	move
	shenti	dwelling in, living in			apta	acquaint, judge
					apt	suck
	atn	a substance			abu	extend
	Kab	a liquid, tash			ab	oppose
	nams	a liquid			annu	howl
	peka	a gap			ash	cry, plaint
	stm	stibium			ax	ruler
	hemka	jasper			abh	wish, favor
	asu, amnu, at, axu	servant, satellite 10 / captain / laborer, follower, compan. / spirit, light			hanp	to spy, a deserter
	asi	noble			ha	hasten
	matti, anti, amuti, apa, as, axu, a	troops, mercenaries / men of the gate / a little / ancestor / noble, great / statue / bow maker / I, me, my, myself			ham hamt	to roar
					huter	to order
					her	silence
					kar	fault
					mat	reverence
					mahaut	homage, obey
						Living persons
					ari	to guard, to keep, companion
					hems, tka, hft, kbu, besht, nini, at	of peaceful action / to sit / to prostrate / to squat / miserable / to revolt, to rebel / quiet, rest / labor produce.
					suax, sbau	to adore / to glorify
					mx, mah	archer, Soldier
					xet, abu, heknu, ha, ux	of dance / to sport / to dance / to welcome, to address / Oh! Hail. / to turn
					kat	to build, to labor
					uau	variant of a star

IDEOGRAPHS AND DETERMINATIVES.

	xabu	ellipid 10ceut.		nat	to knead
	sbau xeft	a convict - impious enemy		beshlu uhu	weak prisoner
	nub netki.	to gild to work in gold.		beshlu uhu	weak prisoner
	ha aau	to rejoice to adore, praise, exalt		nesh set afa tas ases	slave " ancestor noble to please, acquaint, fill
	hunna tehh	suppliant rejoice		aan hanti hanhan	turn back returner command
	ha en	heh, a trillion years illimitably, for ever		pall epillu sas u mehlu	people intelligent beings people of S. Egypti " " N. "
	hes	to sing			
	amn	to hide		ay oxu	spirit manes
	sxai	a scribe		mahahuit akiu amem mer ast	courtiers' family inferior 3 holders Superintendents of fire
	fa	to bear, to carry		set stu bar satk mha at ass	Typhon Baal Sadok
	shur or sur	to drink			of names of females and Goddesses.
	ab an	pure, priest scribe "			
	Nebeh	libation			
					of parturition
	Siem	a judge		men mena ur xem	to bring up to suckle; a wetnurse to dandle " - to put to sleep
	neham	to save		slesi " ap	to drag along supine "

IDEOGRAPHS AND DETERMINATIVES.

		of	over throw
	Xtb		overthrow
	Xr.shr		smite
	sfx		lay waste
	hefu		growl
	nebbu		to humble
	bukbu		malefactor
	het.mi		obscure
	rebal		rebel, culpable
	Xeft		enemies, the impious
	seb	profane	
	Xebti	transformation	Sha accuse
	tut	image	cru ceremony
	Kars	mummy	Ka aform
		of embalmming	
	aut	matter	
	Xat	a body	
	Kars	embalm	
	hes	obedient	
	ab	form, type, image	
	ax	dead, spirit, type	
	Xtb	tumble	
	pet	heavens, the sky	
	nebkt	to wash gold	
		to swim	
	hi	strike	of construction
	ufa	chastise	12
	xem	build, construct	
	Kat	"	
	hi	strike	
	ufa	chastise	
	ten	bruise	
	amentu	hide	
	balsh	lazy, slow, injure	
	betnu	malefactor	
	aau	joy, acclamation	
	sKa	exalt, praise	
	Ka	bearer, wearer (of dia-dem)	
	Ka	to bear, support, extend Ra who extends the heavens.	
	nini	sprinkle	
	Kebeh	libation	
	sems	older, prince, preferred, adopted	
	Hes	to beg, beseech	
	uxs	create, mould	
	sbau	praise, glorification	
	Xet	invert	
	ba	topsy-turvy	
	nnm	pygmy	
	amn	conceal, envelop	
	hak	captive	
	neter han	high priest	
	annu	to look back	
	satem	listen	
	ab	hear, listen	
	ath	ery, plaint	
	tenh	to bind, of Asiatic captive	

IDEOGRAPHS AND DETERMINATIVES.

		Negro captive 12
		chief
	maan	cattle guard
	xiχi	to whip
	ta Seb	to offer sacrifice „ drink
	maan	cattle feeder, driver
	ma	
	ash pherr	cry, plaint
	aba	to play a game
	Kebeh	libation
	neham	rejoice
	mart bah ax akalu anan hti	powerful servant mow babble, want hoe strike
	set	spill. pour out
	uah Kebeh	pour out, to feed libation
	atn	to beat, to pound

	χa	to measure corn
	hes txen	to sing to play the harp
	hti χotbb	to subdue „ „
	tut	statue
	bu Kes	i metäl (with ▨ as tone) subdue, overcome, van- quish
	herri	Quadrigga
	tut	a statue
	Shr	to terrify
	hur	elder

IDEOGRAPHS AND DETERMINATIVES.

	ślā	prisoner, convey		afita / afiru / afirat / afi	upon earth / palate, edge of life / dedication / forthwith	16.
	ur	elder		her	on, upon, face	
	aht or ahit	assistant priestess		ru	mouth	
	hems	to sit		śtēm / an	stibium / appear, show	17
	xen ru xer xart mpa onxu mararu se xrut ofi an afit amlēn	baby of youth / nursling / child / offspring / to grow / to nurse / youth, hero, Soldier / son / child / move / acquaint, judge / cable, rank		ka an nhas res xtr	to spy / adorn / raise up / suspend / content	heslou,... / ara, to pierce / ... sleep / agt, splendor
	atru	to build, form, create		ari rimi axu	eye / weep / shut the eye, wink	
	atti	to build, form, fashion		atini	build, form, sleep	
	xpr xprtu afi	scarab / earth, world / fly	14	ar artu ar ar at at	author / works / produced by- / to make / passage / frontage	
	ment	bier of embalming	15	armaa	to see	
	menat nent xat śtr kar	repose; death / bier, couch / a body / to lay out / to embalm		rimi rom ari	learn / weep / lament	
	menau	sleep, death		an	precinct	
	ati af afitni ha tatu	head / equal / forehead / face / head of the head	16	an	appear, show	
				atti ja kaka hu	tooth / pay / to chew, gobble up / food	18

IDEOGRAPHS AND DETERMINATIVES.

\		of land, working the earth and of angular objects.		ser	brush, reserve, private, effect, oblique, sacred, involved.
	ta	tooth, earth, to swallow			
	hu	means, taste, perception			
	henb't	fountain		ser	distribute, chosen, holy, venerable
	apt	corner			
	aft	horizon 19			(all of this type seem to have the same value)
	ab	clear			
	abehu	tooth			
,	nu	cultivate		ser	arrange
⌐	tat	give, send 20		meha	leave
—	Kab	arm		xu	rule
=	Kabi	a pair of arms			of painting
{}	Kan	breast		Kar	to fight
	hept	unite		Kat	to contend, to kill
	ann	embrace			
	aKa	divide		ma	directly, presently
	apt	rib			
()	tani	to encircle		mna	to nurse 21
	habtu	to hold together		snKau or shKau	} to suckle
()					labyrinth 22
←	akhut	prepare of power			
	ax	light, honor, suspend		Kar	to rob, entrap, hasten secret, harass, ravish
	aau	reproach		Ker	to hold, possess 24
	auaa	steal, take		uuk	to entice
	aa	knit		Kru	garrison
	aua	captain		Sati	the feet
	aufu	chastise		apu	guide, police
	aut	"		sn	knee
	autu	" length		ret	foot
	au	"		xent	approach
	auai	kidnap, gainsay, catch		uar	leg
—		of peaceful action		bu	"
	Kuhu	shoulder		ar	acre
				around	"
	Xi, Xu	to rule, protect, screen a fan		Suten	lie down
				Kama	terrible, roar
	Xu	to rule		apt	guide, lead, propose
	Xu	to rule		peter	en ta. to kneel

IDEOGRAPHS AND DETERMINATIVES.

	skau tha maken bennu sali	sacrifice drunk, deprive slaughter no, not anihilate	24
	heh ait	of motion wander, search asleep, apace	
	sna yosef hem annu	turn away stop, not go slay rise, hold	
	masi	(arne ni) brought, conduct, "les apports", cargo, merchandise	
	art	of parts of the body rump	25
	lash	fleshy part	26
	shaa aau	to be born, flesh sholder	27
	ha ka ua han embak harmata	husband bull ass husband before, in presence foreskin of males	28
	sa han	of the body side binds, strands	29
	ab abu	a game of chess Numidian goat	30
	asui	testes	31
	htar desm rmi	horse mare cattle	32

sam bam	horse	
aua ka aka	bull fat	of cattle
ah aua maht kau	cow white antelope cow	
abhem aua hnhr huau ab	calf steer calf thirst	
salf ba	thigh cow	
sha fonti sesn rex xenn sen	nostril of breathing nose breathe joy sleep breathe	
reru yau asha	boar sow hog	
ab kamer apt ses teb xener ab hali leher	elephant of quadrupeds camel Thebes, hippopotamus askin sandal casque a piece of linen, pied bellows leather	
ba	goat, soul	
serr	Egyptian sheep	
	wild goat	
kax xahsi	gazelle "	
ar at	antellope	
sehak ska sahu	ancestor to collect a crowd race, family, ancestors	

IDEOGRAPHS AND DETERMINATIVES.

	set na	an ass 32 cont.ᵃ		ab	elephant
	uhar	dog		hunz	a wolf
				sa	a fox, a son, an order of priests
	xuu	cat			rhinoceros
	teem	tom-cat		apt	hippopotamus
	maaft	lynx			giraffe
		rat			gryphon
		gerboa rat			sphynx
	aani	ape priest		emsuh ati ayem ati	crocodile extinguish lay out
	hati	worship		sati	connection, beam
	Kant	rage		anx an	hare being, existence
				apsh	tortoise
				hek	frog, numerous
	Seb ansh	jackal, crafty, cunning. magus wolf, dog		ashu	tadpole, many, numerous, million
					innumerable, more than 10.000
				fnti	blind worm
	maau	lion		axu or ashu	lizard, numerous, to supply, to give breath to.
	Sen	lioness, turn back		serk	scorpion

IDEOGRAPHS AND DETERMINATIVES.

hem or samhem	Locust or grasshopper	32 cont.
het Xep hab	bee wasp King of W.r L Egypt	
af	fly	
	mantis	
shft tenln Xeft Xex beb ahit am	ram, to fashion to rise up, pride, revolt demon, liar the throat the gullet the windpipe to eat	33
slà	to conduct	
shft tenth Xeft seshi Nefau	ram, to fashion to rise up, pride demon, liar place in writing desolation	
ah	flesh	
	thirsty	
	dorcas goat	
sekti apehpeh	vigilant gigantic	
Kenbet	subject, servant	
Kfu tenln Xept Nefa emNefau	disturb, hunt rise up, pride thigh seize on the contrary	35

sotem alh	(a sort ear) listen, heard penetrate, regulate	36
besiu tehan	pass elevate, promote	37
palu	mortals	
mut	die	
Kaf enKaf tah tut ta or tam ant	carry bear off steal claw	
Xpsh	a thigh · of fame	38
	a span measure	39
rehat	lord	40
se Xhr sinn Xenn Kai	son, daughter scarab destroy elevate title	
tai	half	
bau	souls	
ta	seize grasp	
ru tarp sent	duck Kind of duck to prove, fear, terror, timid	
hat	beginning	
abhubah bah abahu	bird on corn heap inundation, to swill, harvest. fill, inundate, supply. to gorge	
pat tennu ser maten Hem	to fly to move Kind of goose facilitate create, produce	

IDEOGRAPHS AND DETERMINATIVES.

	Translit.	Meaning		Translit.	Meaning
	ur	of evil		akam	wrapped up
	ulū	sparrow		asham	eagle or falcon
	an	little, deficient, vain		ast	to frighten, to protect
	ak	starve, hurt		tasher	an adjutant, red
	ban	unclean		hem	to find / of seeking
	benai	waste, void, cease			
	bek	cease, depress			
	but	abominable			
	fennu	filthy, dirty		ba	soul
	fekti	evade		sex	nest, waterplace, to fill
	fekar	starve, famish		seshi	nest, marsh, nett
	han	envy, malice		rex	pure, soul, dream
	han nui	conspire			
	hesm	suffocate		rex	pure, soul, dream
	haiu	destroy		rex / rexiu	pure, spirit, wise / intelligent, reasoning beings
	hat	fear		ut / neh	belonging to / drag, agitate
	het	oppress			
	hut	afflict			
	xen	little		anti	the perfume of Anti
	xepen	"		ha	predecessor
	her	false		ba	soul
	emsah	mislay			
	mas	halt			
	mahau	officer's family			
	mayare	desolate			
	anbu	thorn			
	xen / kam	agitate, dilligent; fell, fearful			
	tennu	to move			
	rex	pure, spirit, dream			
	ba / an / aba	soul, spirit / be / pass through, opposite			
	am / amma / shem / fam	give / find / strangle, bind / wicked, match			
	hnua	to fish			
	Mut / atmu	mother / food of the dead			
	tafau	teal or small duck			
	tef	fragrance			
	sek / ba / s'baat / setet	to be idle (snared bird) / " " " / " " " / to tremble			

40 cont.

IDEOGRAPHS AND DETERMINATIVES.

	apt	duck	41
	nrau	to vanquish	
	ħan	number, numerous	
	țenħ	wing	of flying 42
	pai	to fly	
	aẋ	to mount	
	aẋm	to soar	
	țema	to swoop	
	aẋu	to rise, to fly	
	aẋai	to fly	
	aẋeẋ	" "	
	ẋu	wing or plume	
	rm	ray	of fishes 43
	bat	abominable	
	abut	a kind of fish	
	ħukĕr	" " "	
	an	a perch	
	bes	to bring over.	
	anru	gale	
	ẋept	thigh	
	ẋept	shame	
	ẋa	body	
	ru	snake	44
	mehn	asp	
	fnti	worm, viper	
	refref		
	apap	elevate	
	aħt	appophis	
	sba	wicked	
	beṭsh	abomination	
	aẋeẋ	dragon	
	aẋine	fantastic, shame	
	nak	Nak, the great devourer	
	ẋefti	enemy, accuser	
	ħati	fore head.	

	of names of goddesses		
	ura	uraeus	
	mashau	uncertain	
	mehaua	serpent	
	apt	head	
	aŕt	eye	
		of names of trees	
		sycamore	45.
		ash	
	ash	acacia	
		cedar	
		of wood	
	shaua	persea (wood) tree	46
	țr	a shoot, time	47
	ħĕr	horse	
	petĕr	to shew	
	renpa	to increase, grow, plants	
	ẋer	youthful.	
	teo	he, it, they	
	suten	king	
	aẋm	to grow	of plants
	dmu	a flower	48
	herri		
	aṛp	vine	
	uehm	maize	
	ħu	corn.	
	mħa	dates	
	bĕt	corn, barley	
	mahu	crown of flowers	
	ħan	field	
	menhi	fodder, clover	
	mash		
	aalu	food	(lotus)
	sem	reeds	
	aak	fodder	
	menhi	clover, fodder	
	herer	a flower	
	su	wheat	
	boti ħut	white barley, wheat	

IDEOGRAPHS AND DETERMINATIVES.

		delicious 48 con!
	ih	nosegay
	aar	a vine
	benr	dates, palm tree, delight
	ash	acacia, cedar
	´	a kind of nosegay
		lotus emblem of L.E.
	xa	to rejoice
	asx	to reap
		delicious
		(lotus leaves)
		(a pod or lotus leaves)

	xa	a title
	raska	joy
	rsh	joy
		a material of stone
	mka or men	to pound, pace, go round
	ashe	alaburnam
	arr	grapes 49
	rnpa	dates
	ba	bronze
	ret	a turnip, boat
	anem	pearl, jasper 50
	ant	kind of unguent, yellow
	anli	perfume
	Kar	horizon of cities 51
	merr	a cake
	nut	a city
		new morr
	ta	stick 52
	ba	bough, wood
	hebni	ebony
	markabuta	chariot
	nsr	paddle
	usr	„ „
	Kar	a bolt
	at	lintel
	mqa	balance
	xa	wood, stick, sceptre
	aaut	pike
	aat-Ka	uta. a sledge, a chariot
	aft	abode, couch
	at	kind of wood
	asr	tamarind wine
	akara	bolt
	absi	part of a boat
	aaut	a boat
	aker	viper
	ams	hold a stick
	ben ben	palm branch
	bolau	holes for ropes
	hata	a mat, a bed
	han	a stick
	hakr	applied to festivals
	hqka	a grove
	ari	lintel
	ash	acacia. cedar
	naxt	power
	xet	afterwards

IDEOGRAPHS AND DETERMINATIVES.

𓏏	ta	a stick	53		arr xent ab ha	steps, to mount, a hall. an approach a flower " "	58
					makfh an	a stand, a frame, stocks ascend	
𓏲	ta	a club			xekt hri hati	a tomb (a tomb door) to fear afraid	59
	ha	abode	54				
	neter ha	temple			ha	a palace, a house	60
	maten her sher ar	park, road, way, path road to approach to guide to go to reach	55		hait	ceiling	61
	annu ha	four time o'day			ha ak rehi	palace house garden	62
	sebti anbu ab and maten	wall wall of enclosure, rampart cornice a path	56		usex	Hall of the two Truths	63
	xem xem	to bruise, to crush				Pylon	64
	maklun	a tower				Propylon	65
					sebxt	gate	66
	per	of house & its parts a house	57		ar han an arru neh arrut	hall to bend, relations a hall " to form, to execute to struggle, to oppose	67
	per hut	treasure house			mer	a circuit, an enclosure	68
	hu	house			anbu	wall of enclosure, enclosed names of prisoners enclosed	69
	ruper	temple			an ru an hu sex marbet	a door, a hatch cover a door to open shut a boat's hatch	70
	ha nub	house of Gold, or Hall of Gold: i.e. Hall of death					

IDEOGRAPHS AND DETERMINATIVES.

⊓	serx	door, pylon	71	🚤	sti sebkt ha	cabin " slip
⚒	axet sxeb	fowler, weaver, artisan join. slab	70	⛵	sesn sesrt ses nef tepak takai fa	sail air breathe breath, air, wind snow to sail to carry
▬ ▭	mua hit iuma alr merut	water ocean sea river lake	73	🐦		
mer	mer afru alu axm hiuu hau meri	basin, lake river, distance river, measure bank, wave inundate territory beloved of -		🛶	ta xeref	to sail to stop
▭	aunara teb ka ab kat	of stone & minerals stone, pebble brick a (brick floor) a drachm	74	⛵	sti sebkt	cabin
⚕	heb	festival, panegyric	75	⛵	xet	to navigate
⚓	heb hut	festival good dæmon		⌣		archaic form of boat
⋒	heb	festival		🚣	xeref	to stop a boat
⊓	heb	festival		🚢	uaa ba	a big boat
🏵	heb	triumph	76	⛵	ua en Ra	boat of the Sun
🛶	ba uua uex mua mehn auak maat tu xen xef kau fextu	boat " hold barge deck cabin hatches to go by boat to make a boat to stop, to anchor to stay	77	⚓	ua en neter	boat of a God
				🚤		barge of Amen
				🚤		barge of Xons
				🚤		barge of Mut
🛶	neshm	bulwark		🚤		barge of Socaris
🛶	uat sunti xeref hunti	boat to detain to stop a boat; to anchor		⚓	sekket	barge of Ra
				🚤		barge of Socaris
				🛶	ua at	a boat as a satellite

IDEOGRAPHS AND DETERMINATIVES.

	transliteration	meaning	no.
	nuh, Aati, senh, sent, atnu	a cord, lowline, bind, found, to build, to form	78
u	urn	stern	79
Ka	Kam, sba, ta	to create, wicked, fowling stick	80
	heplu	poop-deck	81
	xa en	the wood of the mast	82
	aluka	rigging	83
	bala	blocks	84
	negri	halyards	85
	bast	rowlocks	86
	hems	rudder	87
	hpi	paddle-blade	88
	matbot	hatch cover	89
	usr, hept	oar, paddle	90
	xepsh, xerltb	a sword, to smite, to prostrate	91
	pest, het, pext, peti	yellow paint, to shoot, to extend, black race, Ethiops, Lybians	92
	atnt, pest, peti, ph	refuse, strength, bow, in Stabl	93

	transliteration	meaning	no.
	sast, sati, eti, ser	arrow, shoot, arrow, arrow-head	95
	Kaut, meny, Kat, meny	fabricate, build, construct, fabricate, work, labor, create, form, an artisan, laborers, soldiers or other tools	96
	Kat, hon hu, serka, Kas, Kers, ab, bena	inscription, phallus, to carve, to embalm, a coffin, ivory work, palm branches	97
	Nen	a little	
	hui	a mace	
	us	a saw	98
sh	srha, art, sefer, xer, ark, ar, anh, anb, shom, anx, hab, henx, mer, Kras, seeht, hap, hau, am, Xeft	aroll, a papyrus, a package, a bag, to tie, to fall down, binding, clothes, clothes, nosegay, list, each, every, strap, dress, clothes, reckon, account, a girdle, bind, embalm, a ship, to hide, to be naked, cloak, clothes	99
	ant, xetma, senns, sens	a ring, to shut, to enclose, to turn away	100
	sesh	a ring, a handle	
	at, sah, xi	a circle, times, the ego, person,	101

IDEOGRAPHS AND DETERMINATIVES.

	sha sna matiu	(a seal ring) to encase to turn away, knee repose, quiet, dead, precept	102		an ab kabalu korali	homed pur horns two horns	112
	pesh pexra pxa pxat	(half cartouche) to separate divisions rod lioness	103		nub	gold of god enamel	113
	menat xet	seal seal, shut	104		mahr henher	mirror "	114
	heha habu heny hap aft at huth at	(basket and cord) of clothing naked to clothe a girdle conceal cartonnage cup table cloth a kind of linen	105		sba merh as	a flail beast, servant, mole, sepulchre, chamber, tomb, idleness, fault, leisure	115
	xat hes hebs abu bot sta hu hes naha ashahu bat bekannu fenka neh hi kekar arar	of foul things mummy embalm wrap, reckon, account elephantia bad, evil, abominable to conduct filthy " foul, copros ashes food, rations malefactor to evacuate foul impurity hunger, starve seed	107		xa boti	to measure corn barley	119
					hat hept stobexen	half pint of measure	120
					ak tfu kufni ya boti hept hes shenef	bread fragrance " food corn, barley solid food	121
					nehar ta	a kind of bread a heap	122
	ant xesbet kam shebet xesbet-ma	of metals, colors, gems, parfume yellow blue - artificial lapis lazuli jasper porcelain lapis lazuli	108		lesr	a plate, a liquid, cream or cheese	123
	han kara	of boxes a box sarcophagus, shrine	109		ten sen utau	a name to bind, an orbit a pendant	124
	xem kars	a box, a shrine embalmment, funeral	110		Pet Het Barnu an	Nubia upper Egypt Barnea to return	125
	tab kars qa	(a bed) a box a coffin bier	111				

IDEOGRAPHS AND DETERMINATIVES.

	mer hab yebua ba bamt	to love, beloved plough (to plough) to hoe a hoe to glide	126
	hab yebua habut her ska amer	a plough to plough ein ebony to harrow to plough a storehouse	127
	asex artt	a sickle, to reap buttock	128
	hesep or lat'a	a nome	129
	sersh aat hi	a standard a standard a place to draw	130
	uax pekau	a marsh a shape	131
	shiu	standards	185
	as aptu or abtu	work, skill to lay foundation	136
		lunar standard	187
	uxt	power	188
			189

		inverted horns seven horns blank writing material misdress of writing name of a goddess	140
	tes uts res enhas emhas res uts	(balance post) to transport to carry, to go out to suspend to excite to arouse to watch to lift, examine, suspend	141
	maha	balance	142
		scale	
	sexex	to balance, adjust	143
	ta tam tkai	a finger to bear to adhere	144
	sex matt	to examine	145
		of foreign land	
		of foreign people	
	ta tka pett	(a hook) to bear away to adhere ready	146
	ulen habt teb	(gilded band of metal) consecration a fold, redoubled	147
	atbu utn men mena len tebenben ser	wells ingot, weight go round to pound to circulate " " s'élancer	148

IDEOGRAPHS AND DETERMINATIVES.

	heq, ami, naxb	a crook rule, a crook a ruler a title, to inscribe 149		aa it	dew paint, to figure	
	snab	back of a chair health 150		set	palm measure	
	uga	strength 151				161
	max au max hema	a key, ripe, blest blest is, mature is hemp 152		pest "	back spine	162
	ta	the earth, the land 157				163
	ta			at tat hetta atti at	substance type, drop, tear type "	164
	tai	Egypt, the land of the winged Sun. id: the two regions, Upper & Lower Egypt		alen	captive	165
	tau	countries		sah ru	gate	166
	hesp	district			leopard's skin	167
	mu	isles		xef shep chef	to receive to take, hold, seize	168
	r em her	mouth (door of the head 158		tat shent ajet arit tattu zet	emblem of stability stability, follow, palette impart bottom establish	169
		ears 159				170
	hfa hep	fist, seize by force hand, fist 160		Shem Xem Xem	bolt, shrine Ichyphallic God	171
	set	palm measure		Xaui ax	altar "	172
	shept shep	hand take			shrine, ark	173

IDEOGRAPHS AND DETERMINATIVES.

	xaiu	shrine	174			Ordinals	188
	hethu	altar, table of offerings 175				meh-uu first	
	xaui	altar	176			meh-sen second	
	xaa	altar	177			meh-xem third	
	xaiu	altar	178			mehftaa fourth	
	xaui	altar	179			meh-seb fifth	
	xau	altar	180			meh-sas sixth	
						meh-sfx seventh	
	axa arit	censer staircase, hall	181			meh-xaut eighth	
		(breast, arms and paddle) is placed	182			meh-psit ninth	
	lent					meh-met tenth or —	
	asha Sem	field clover	183			meh-ua first	
	sha	a field	184			meh-sen second	
	xersa	a truss of hay	185			mehxem third	
						mehftaa fourth	
	shenti	living in, dwelling in.	186			meh-seb fifth	
						meh-sas sixth	
						mes-sfx seventh	
						meh-xaut eighth	
						meh-psit ninth	
						meh-met tenth	
						set five	
						met-psit, 19	
						fime-psit 49	
						tut seb 25	
						ashu thousands, or very many	
	Paut	divine assembly of the Gods Synod of the Gods	187			" numerous (oxen & geese)	
						" " (honors)	

IDEOGRAPHS AND DETERMINATIVES.

	Transliteration	Meaning	No.
	sep ua	once	188
	sep sen	twice	
	sep xem	thrice	
	sep ftua	four times	
	sessennu	thousandth	
	ua ment, met, u	thousands	
	hu	tens thousands	
	sshu	hundreds thousand	
		millions	
	mha	billions	
		all time, forever	
	Teta	everlasting, zero, infinity	
	api	first	
	"	"	
	"	"	
	Ki	second	
	lā	(a stick or club)	189
	tex	a weight, a supply of liquid	190
	sesha	a shekel	191
	Tat	(a buckle)	192
	armas	(two eyeballs) to see	193
	ai	to go	194
	aa annu	to bring tribute, tribute	195
	sam "	to direct, pass, traverse; a statue	196
	apeh	hall, floor; circular, to encircle	197
	perai	to go out	198
	hen Kapa	to sing; to fumigate	199
	ab aslat shua ma abu ab ab	a kind of wine; a seat or throne; right, proper; pure, clean; feast	200
	shes	to serve, a fellow, a servant	201
	balā ba bu	gift (a sledge & stone); reward; bestow, symbol of the product of riches	202
	mer	a chest, box, ring	203
	akm	(a shield)	204

IDEOGRAPHS AND DETERMINATIVES.

	neft sirui	fan, flabellum a fan	205
	at	hear, words	206
	at nemi	fish	207
	shuam ah ma ohu	feather, with, at dream exempt	208
	xem sept	prevail lighten	209
	a ab	pass, oppose	210
	ab Kam	material	211
	artu	bullock	212
	anla at	hour of the day minute	213
	ahr	equip	214
	ain	create, reckon	215
			216
	hen hen	a packet "	217
	benben	cap, tip, roof	219
	hi hi	to drag	220

	het ti	soles of the foot	221
	hankh Kaf	throat, change desolate	222
	hankh	throat, change	223
	hut	silver	224
	hut	a mace	
	hutu	onions	225
	Aut	while	226
	amo	hold a stick	227
	hut	onion	228
		sceptre of lower Egypt	229
	usef	fiat, decree, station	230
	Sxem	germ	
	aau aaiu aat	labor, work, honor, glory, title artisan, dignity	231
	suten rech	King of upper Egypt	232
	nema uat	to force to turn back to make grow	233

IDEOGRAPHS AND DETERMINATIVES.

	lif anhater nap	in tera time lark grain	234		bok	cutn (heap)	250
	lab	a fig	235		hut	onions (bundle of)	251
		(a pomegranite)	236			pylon, gate	252
	han ar	a box grapes	237		Xara	a chest	253
		vertebra	238		ast hes Kat hesb	a throne, a place " " a throne, a seat	254
	ala	slay	239		ten ast aset Asir	a seat a place, situation Isis Goddess Osiris God.	255
	hanna henbi	a well territory	240		sebt	dog star, Sothis	256
	serh ssau	drain floor	241		texen tehen texen xai	Obelisk " engraved Obelisk	257
	mer	2nd class cities, and water stations				lotus bud capital column	258
	ashr	slice	242			lily lotus capital column	259
	ba	captive, prostrate, to conduct	243			lily lotus capital column	
	ba herni	iron salt				down palm capital column	
	em kefau	on the contrary	244		nuper	temple	260
	em nem ushem	again, repeat to renew	245		kani	chair	261
	Xem	hemp	246		hes Ka Kat	sofa throne, seat	262
	hma	flax	247				
	snut	granary	248				
	nam	block, place of execution	249				

IDEOGRAPHS AND DETERMINATIVES.

	ulā	palanquin	263		het	crown of upper Egypt	280
		(a seat)	264				281
		(a chapel)	265				282
	an anru	total, account a stone	266		texh	crown of lower Egypt	283
	Kar Nell	a furnace	267		xeperah	helmet	284
	hai	a tablet	268		nams	a wig	285
	hab	a shrine	269		nams	a wig	286
		fill, inundate	270		abeb baba	horns, extremities, a tip	287
	neph	a potter's stand, to mould	271		tas teau	the tie of the crown to raise, elevate	288
	apt	a manger, Thebes	272		ub usex	a collar	289
	Aurs huls ulā	a pillow	273		xasx	a collar	290
	xar	load	274		shena	a collar	291
	arrt	crown with asps	275		xax	a collar	292
	mahu	chaplet, crown	276		annua	to tie up, plain	293
		crown, circlet	278		usex	a collar	294
		crown of flowers	279		men	a bracelet, an anklet	295
					men	a bracelet, an anklet	296

IDEOGRAPHS AND DETERMINATIVES.

	ula	a pectoral plate	297		tkh	a shoe latchet	309
	maka	a metallic anklet	298		sersh	a sistrum player an assistant priestess	310
	ash	a string of beads, Acacia or cedar gum	299		sersh	a sistrum to play the sistrum	311
	shent	an apron	300		sersh	sistrum	312
	sha	armor	301				
	shua sem	a plume a feather	302			occurs in Louvre papyrus as " — au" an ingredient in an ointment for the memory	313
					xex pexa	a whip to whip	314
					sba ata menx	a prop uten ells	315
	atef	the Crown of Osiris and of Gods of Lower world	303				316 (a stick)
	atef	Crown of Horus	304		Kannu Tema	hemp stands linen cloth	317
					tahen	crystals	318
		chain armor	305		aka aku	a battle axe	319
	teb tebtu tebteb	sandal two sandals sandals	306		neter neter han	a god a high priest, prophet	
	xaibt	a fan, refuse	307		xetni	a battle axe	320
	ser	a fly flap	308		anext	a wood man's axe	321

IDEOGRAPHS AND DETERMINATIVES.

	baasu	a dagger 322			in overseer of the... 335
	xaa	a dagger, a chief, above, first 323		sat	336
	hurr	a chariot 324		ela sat salu	a ball of thread, to low, to spin, to lead, to convey. to lead a cord 337 (a reel & cord)
	grai	to write, a scribe, painting 325			
		scribes' pallet 326			
					to reel cord & twine 338
	ux	a weigt, appointed 327			a spindle 339 to establish to prepare name of a metal
ma	ma xena	a reed pen 328 to shut, to seperate, a concubine		ab alin ax afr neit Net	a papyrus roll. oppose form light equip things letter 340
	ur	in quantity of food, fruit.			
tam	tam sert sem	scepter 329 a liquid, cream or butter gold			
	user	power, victory, riches 330		terut	a roll of papyrus 341
	uabt	the West 331			a chisel 342
	shaa les per tait	book 333 tied up roll house of books, library			(linen bands) 343
		(a polisher) shadow(?) 333		aat	a closed net 344
	ab arf	food, cook 334 bag, pouch, purse		raat	a net 345
				aat	an expanded net 346

Symbol	Transliteration	Meaning	No.		Symbol	Transliteration	Meaning	No.
	hat, aat	chaos, a net	347				a basketful of cakes	361
	setp	to judge, to select, to approve	348				(of extent; width, space	362
	tua, uuha	to return, retake, escape, fisherman (boat & net)	349				a cake	363
			350			nebet	date cake	364
	ab, an, hentu	in dumb, an animal, Heliopolis, arms, idols, with nails. Is much elongated in the t. as reliefs; Is probably one of the masts raised in honor of the Gods	351			Kabi	honey comb, a quarter of an aroura of land	365
			352			pu, "	a shutter, a mat	366
		(incense burner)	353			ben, nebi, rub, ayu, heon, bat, er, Sak	dates, to germinate, censer, honey, conserve, fruit, barley, since, to collect	367
	alt, mals	enclose, select, whip	354					368
	sahu, sab	received, constellation of Orion	355			neb	lord	369
	sah	Orion, assemble, perambulate, a journey	356			Neb er	tr. lord of all, universal God	
	nena		357			ba	iron, cloud (a crucible)	370
							archaic form of crucible	371
	sep	times	358			aten, Har	tank, rank, curve	372
	stem	stibium	359				(an emblem of Suphis)	373
	at	bread	360			u	one, line, edge	374
						sens	food, a ragout	375
						ta, art	to give, termination of present participle	376
						neter atet	incense	377
								378

IDEOGRAPHS AND DETERMINATIVES.

	transliteration	meaning	no.		transliteration	meaning	no.
	pet, fa	a bowcase, to remain	379		amen (ensa men), hemi	(ensa men)	393
	soah	a journey	380		betsh	lazy, slow, revolt	394
	sent, sennt	foundation, to found	381	tem	tem	total	395
	tatau	proper, peculiar (from tata, prince, minister, chief) (abbreviation of 129.)	382		het	half	396
			383		hat	heart	397
			384		sept, septi	lip, banks, shores	398
	nemt	gallows, block	385		hem	female	399
	shat, ashen, asex, hebt, hent, hesb, heska, mati, ma	cut, stab, mow, cast out, cut, rub, destroy, desolation, cut, cut, hard, thick, cut	386	hetep	hetep	a table, peace, offerings, food, goods	400
	au	joy, magnanimity	387		tet	dish	401
	ma net sep	continued	388		ast	a rope	402
			389		nnush, nnushem, nashem	rib, kidney, liver, loin	403
	nas, ax, nasr, "	tongue, adore, superintendent, a chief	390		smat	daub the eyebrow, stibium, half month	404
	apr	to equip	391		sept	shore, lip, margin	405
	an	a whetstone, to order, to dispose	392		ua, Kama	sole, only, one, lake	406
				t	het	small (a muller)	407
					hen	of ivory earring	408
					kar	tail	409

IDEOGRAPHS AND DETERMINATIVES.

	sem, mali pen	of things divided, such as, straw, bristles, fodder &c. back 410 neck back, spine
	smenx	work, utensils 411
	ru tli satu	door gate a festival 412
	net	Knead, address, save, help, afflict, punish, hail! homage, praise to. glory to. 413
	mena	to sharpen, to cut 414
	pebu sexa	a leather cutter to make 415
	uah	crown, buckle 416
	pesm per	a cake a kind of cake 417
	ru	a spike 418
	sxa ker	to embellish 419
	nefer	food, youth, merit, beauty worth, to ornament. 420
	solem	to hear 421
	utau	pectoral plate 422
	tens uteb	part of a net; a stretcher to stretch 423
	xaka	to shave 424
	urx ashab	a clepsydra 425

	gret	to squeeze, to make bread 426
	sha sken	to rise (sun rising) a cake, kind of food 427
		428
	ber ber	a pyramid 429
	hankti sen xam amen akab rut	mane, down ideogram a lock, a curl of wrong black of grief wool - evil 430 grief - of torment posterity
	ret rut	race (a sling) engrave 431
		(counterpoise for collar) 432
		433
		434
		435
	nub	gold 436
		437
		438

IDEOGRAPHS AND DETERMINATIVES.

Sign	Name	Meaning	No.		Sign	Name	Meaning	No.
			439			menti	the two mountain chains bordering the Valley of the Nile	455
			440			Sah	constellation of Orion	456
			441			sen ua sepsen sepsenut	once twice thrice	(indicates that the preceeding word must be repeated) (2d) 457
	nemb		442					
	ba	a basket	of mines and quarries 443				follows ha-nub, House of Gold aneuphuism used by the Egyptians to avoid the mention of Death.	458
							is probably a variant of the same.	
	hems hemet	to sit a wife, woman	444					459
	ab aba peka	purification against, contrary a gap	445					460
	ma	a cubit, a forearm's length just, true	446			per xentu	harem, house of concubines	461
	am	(capstone over gate)	447				ruins	462
	Ngt		448				ruins	
	xen	(a swamp or morass) a swamp, morass	449				head of an enemy, an Asiatic	463
	xabes	a beard	450			ba	bronze	464
	sek	a battle axe	451			butau	a piece of wood of the sacred boat.	465
	sek	to seize	452					466
		a suspended vase	453			set	to impregnate, to shoot arrows, to throw bread on the ground, to pour libations	467
	shes	to serve	454					

IDEOGRAPHS AND DETERMINATIVES.

			468
			469
		One of the Cabiri	470
	ba	the soul	471
	neferu	graces, merits, beauties, excellencies	472
		a symbol of Osiris	473
		a fingers' breadth, ¼ of a hand's breadth, ⅟₂₈ of a cubit, ⅟₂₄ of a royal cubit	474
		two fingers breadth	
		three fingers breadth	
		a hand's breadth	475
		five fingers breadth	
		six fingers breadth	
		seven fingers breadth	
		eight fingers breadth	
		a span	476
	au	a cubit, 24 fingers brdth	

SYMBOLS.

	Xat nint	Kings chamberlain			priest of Anubis
	neter nefer	good god			ascribe
	neter ba	holy soul		ab	Priesthood, purity
	neter hat, annu	horoscope			liturgies
	suten neter meri	King god-beloved a priest			prayer
	neter suten han	the god his majesty. a priest		sba en Ra / anet en Ra	Praised to Ra!
		a priest			prayer
		a priest		tat net	gift to a god
		high priest of Amen			offerings to the temple
		title of a priest. of Neith			foar
		Priestess of Pthah			offering of oxen & geese
		a female musician, a priestess			Vases of the Temple, things dedicated
		sculptors		hetepu	things dedicated
	shes	servants, or some kind of priests followers.		Mek nu	holy water, magic water
	sheou	servants			sacrifices

SYMBOLS

Symbol		Meaning	Symbol		Meaning
		sacrifices			temple
		meat offering			temples
		offering of lotus flowers			"
		offering of pomegranite			"
		offering of olive oil			"
		id			"
		sacred loaves, consecrated cakes			a shrine or portable temple
	neter hau	temples			a shrine, a temple
	kar neter	hades			a great house, a temple
		"			" " " "
		"			a temple, a libation house
		house of the Gods			" " " "
		scribe of the temple			temple of Ptah
		palace, Kings' house			" " "
		Kings house, temple			" " "
		house of gold, hall of death			temple in the city of Ptah or Memphis
		seat or place of the lord			temple of Ra in the city of the sun, Heliopolis, Thebes
		sanctuaries of Thebes Temple			a temple
		"			a temple
		"			
		seats, places, temples			

SYMBOLS.

Symbol	Transliteration	Meaning	Symbol	Transliteration	Meaning
	suten ha	palace of the King		Tex pehent	King of L.E.
	ha ur	house of Nea, Truth Great house of the Gods			King of U. & L.E.
	mi amon	Ramases, Memnonium			Queen of U.E.
		the Memnonium			Queen of U.E.
	sekhet	a walled court			Queen of L.E.
		a walled court			the lord the King of U.E.
		temple services			the lord the King of L.E.
		"			King Ruler of U.E.
		"			King Ruler of L.E.
		"			King governor of U. & L.E.
		"			the queen of U. & L.E.
		Offerings, purification			the King of the land; the two eyes represent the portals of the Nile.
		"			King of L.E.
		"			King of U. & L.E.
		sacrifices,			King of U. & L.E
		sacrifices, gifts for			His Majesty
		King of U.E.			His Majesty the King
					His Majesty the King
					heavenly King
					the queen
					King
					King & queen

SYMBOLS

Symbol	Transliteration	Meaning
	se Ra	son of Ra
	set Ra	daughter of Ra
	suten xabt	King of the two regions
	suten reshu	King of L.E.
		offerings
		illustrious
		servant, one of the four orders of priests
		"
		"
		"
		.
		"
	neb	lord
	nebt ha	the lady of the house
	neb ha	the master of the house
	neb reshu	lord of L.E.
	neb meht	lord of W.E.

Symbol	Transliteration	Meaning
	neb tu u	lord of battles, conqueror
	neb xepsh	lord of the sword
	neb xam	lord of Egypt
	shent Kau	Ruler of the countries
	neb tau	lord of lands
	neb xeperi	lord of the two Egypts
	neb tai	queen of the two countries
	nebt tai	queen of the two countries
	neb t Ha tai	lady of the throne of the two countrys
	neb sha	lord of the field
	neb Abt	lord of W.E. or Thebes
	nu reshu	land of the South, U.E.
	nu meht	land of the North, L.E.
	reshu mehtu	} North & South Egypt
	aah	the moon
	aahu	months, in describing a person's age
	aah	id:
		monthly
		a fortnight or half month
		id
	uak	a week

SYMBOLS

Calendars

(symbol)	thoth	season of vegetation the month of		*(symbol)*	paoni	the month of	
(symbol)	paophi	"	"	"	*(symbol)*	epep	"	"	"
(symbol)	athyr	"	"	"	*(symbol)*	mesore	"	"	"
(symbol)	choac	"	"	"	*(symbol)*	tobi	harvest months
(symbol)	tybi	harvest months	*(symbol)*	mechir	the month of
(symbol)	mechir	month of	*(symbol)*	phamenoph	"	"
(symbol)	phamenoth	"	"	*(symbol)*	pharmuthi	"	"
(symbol)	pharmuthi	"	"	*(symbol)*		season of vegetation, or first third of the civil year
(symbol)	pachon	season of the rise of the Nile	*(symbol)*	thoth	the month of
(symbol)	payini	the month of	*(symbol)*	thoth	"	"	"
(symbol)	epiphi	"	"	*(symbol)*	paophi	"	"	"
(symbol)	mesore	"	"	*(symbol)*	tobi	"	"	"
(symbol)	thoth	flowering months	*(symbol)*	tobi	"	"	"
(symbol)	paophi	the month of	*(symbol)*	mechir	"	"	"
(symbol)	athor	"	"	"	*(symbol)*		season of inundation
(symbol)	choak	"	"	"	*(symbol)*	pachon	the month of
(symbol)	pachon	season of the rise of the Nile	*(symbol)*	paoni	"	"	"
			(symbol)	paoni	"	"	"
			(symbol)	epep	"	"	"

SYMBOLS.

Symbol	Transliteration	Meaning		Symbol	Zodiac
	sjiep	month of			star of darkness
	mesore	"			star of darkness
	hru	a day			star of light
		" "			
		first day			star of light
	annu	hour			
	annut	the appointed hour			star of light
	"	" " "			Aries
	"	" " "			Taurus, the birth or rising of Taurus
		planets or wandering stars			Taurus
	hru	evening star			Taurus
	aba Karh	j star of night			Taurus
		star of night			Orion
					Gemini
		star of night			Gemini
		star of night			Gemini
					Gemini
		star of night			Sothis
					the heliacal rising of the Dog Star

SYMBOLS.

Symbol		Meaning	Symbol		Meaning
		Leo			water processions
		Libra			bridge
		Libra			the two doors of heaven
	Serk	Scorpio			the two doors of the Nile
		boat of Ra			the keeper of the two doors
		aquarius			door keeper
		chief, or first			door keeper
		chief, or last			door keeper
		master of the house			guardian of the door
		id " " "			jewels
		chief of the temple			treasures
		id " " "			treasures
		chief of the great house		Semkat	silver
		chief of the temples		mesu Kat	silver
		chief scribe			mines
		chief priest			mines
		chief of the learned men			mines
		chief			mines
		captain of soldiers			money
					debt

SYMBOLS.

Symbol		Meaning	Symbol	Phonetic	Meaning
		treasury		mayt	blessed
		paid, remitted			id:
		money			id:
		id:			conqueror
		id:			lord of the years
		id:			id: · · ·
		id			victories
		money, to pay, to sell.			savior, defender, avenger, punisher
		money, gifts to the temple			defender
					hero
		money, gifts to the temple			hero
					friendship
		chariot		setp en	approved, chosen by
		belonging to - of		meri en	beloved of -
		master		mer	beloved of -
		mistress			seen, shewn, "so that it may be seen that it is lawful."
		master			seen, shewn
		master of the land			proclamation
		id: · · ·			id
		belonging to the temple, a title of Neith			honor
		righteous			honor
		blessed			gave victory

SYMBOLS.

		gives life			to clothe
		give blessing		ha	to set up an Obelisk. to load a ship
		give royally		s'ha	to cause to be set up
		everlasting, eternal immortality		perei	going out
	mezt	blessing		un	to bear patiently
	maxe neb	all blessed		hru en sha	accession day
		conqueror			regulator or alderman to make, to fashion
		id,			regulating the rites
		slave			perform
	Kanext	powerful bull			archaic form of man squatting
	mexeru	justified, justifier			lord of the enemies
		justified			soldiers
	Xat	deceased			archer
		raised			castle
		righteous			king of W. of Egypt
		grey, spotted			eldest son
	tesher	red			progenitors, ancestors
		white		alef alef	grandfather
	Xemv	black			great grand father
		wore the redment			

SYMBOLS.

	mut	mother	
	naut	mother	
	alĕf mut	alĕf mut	
	henut	wife	
	shent	sister, Kinswoman.	
	shen	brother, Kinsman.	
		id	"
	shent	sister	
	shent mut	aunt	
	shent en alĕf set	neice	
	set shent en mut	cousin	
		a filthy man, (hog)	

GRAMMAR.

	Articles				Pronoun
	Pa	the, masculine		entuf	he
	Pai	the, "		entus	she
	ta	the, feminine		entset she	she
	tai	the, "		entketen	you
	na	the, plural		entsen	they
	nai	the, "		entu	they
		Demonstrative pronouns			**Pronoun suffixes**
	pui	this, these, masc:		a	I,
	pfi	this "		a	I,
	tui	this, these fem:		k	thou, masc:
	tfi	this "		t	thou, fem:
	pen	this, these, masc: } both			these suffixes have no independent existence as words: When affixed to nouns they have the force of possessive pronouns; affixed to verbs they become personal pronouns as:
	ten	this, these, fem: } numbers		f	he
	mennu	that, these		s	she
	enen	those, that: precede the noun, the others follow it.		set	she
	pu	This, these, & serves frequent while a substantive verb to connect subject and predicate. Tef-a pu seb "my father the same is Seb"		nu	we
		Personal pronouns		ten	you
	anuk	I,		sen	they
	nuk	I,		set	they
	entuk	thou, masc:		u	they
	entut	thou, fem:		un	they

"Pishu-a ru-a" open I mouth my I open my mouth

GRAMMAR.

	Pronoun			Pronoun	
	anuk	I		entāsen	they
	anuk	I		entāsen	they
	anuk	I, King or God		sen	they
	nuk	I		a	I, me, mine
	nuk	I		a	I, me, mine
	nuk	I		a	I, me, mine, King or God
	nuk	I		a	I, me, mine
	nuk	I King or God.		a	I, me, mine
	nuk	I		kua	I, me, mine
	.nuk	I		ua	I, me, mine
	nuk	I		k	thou, thine
	nuk	I feminine		t	thou, thine fem:
	nuk	I " " "		k	thou, thine
	enták	thou masc:		t	thou, thine fem:
	net	thou fem:		t	thou, thine fem
	entáf	he		f	his, him, his
	su	he (see independent pro:)		u	he, him, his
	entás	she		su	he, him, his
	nen	we		su	he, him, his
	anen	anen		s	she, her
	entulēv	ye		set	she, her
	entulân	ye		seset	she, her
	entân	ye		s	she, her
	entāen	they		set	she, her
				set	she, her
				seset	she, her
				n	we, our, common gender
				nu	we, our " "
				nen	we, our " "
				n	we, our " "

GRAMMAR.

	Pronoun				Pronoun	
	tĕn	he, him, his		pai-a	my, masc: sing:
	tĕn	he, him, his		pai-a	my, " " God, King
	tĕn	he, him, his		pui-a	my, " "
	tĕn	he, him, his		na-a	my, masc: plural
	tĕn	he, him, his		pai-a	my, " "
	u	they, them, their		nai-a	my, " " God, King
	sen	they, them, their		na	my, " " "
	sen	they, them, their			
	set	they, them, their			
	sen	they, them, their		pa-na	our, com: gen: sing:
	sen	they, them, their		pai-na	our " " "
	set	they, them, their		nai-na	our " " plural
	s	they, them, their		pa-k	thy, thine, masc: sing:
		Independent pronouns		pai-k	thy, thine, " "
	til	is used as the French "on" and when applied as a base to the Suffixes produces a Series of Independent pronouns - as		pai-k	thy, thine, " "
	taa	I		pai-k	thy, thine, " "
	tuk	thou		pui-k	thy, thine, " "
	tuf	he		na-k	thy, thine, masc: plur:
	set	an independent suffix		nai-k	thy, thine, " "
	su	he, an independent personal pronoun		nai-k	thy, thine, " "
				nai-k	thy, thine, " "
		Possessive pron:		nai-k	thy, thine " "
	pa-a	my, masc: sing:		pa-t	thy, thine, fem: sing:
	pai-a	my " "		pai-t	thy thine " "

GRAMMAR.

	pait	thy, thine, fem: sing:		pas	her, sing:
	pait	" " " "		pas	" "
	na-t	thy, thine, fem: plu:		pais	"
	nait	" " "		pais	"
	nai-t	" " "		pais	"
	patn	your, masc: sing:		nas	her, plu:
	paṫn	" " "		nas	"
	paṫn	" " "		nais	"
	pait n	" " "		nais	"
	natn	your, masc: plu:		nais	"
	natn	" " "		pasn	their, com: gen: sing
	naitn	" " "		paisn	" " " "
	naitn	" " "		paisn	" " " "
				paisn	" " " "
	paf	his, sing:		paisn	" " " "
	paif	" "		paisn	" " " "
	paf	" "		nasn	their com: gen: plu:
	paif	" "		nasn	" " " "
	puif	" "		naisn	" " " "
	naf	his, plu:		naisn	" " " "
	naif	" "		naisn	" " " "
	naif	" "		naisn	" " " "
	naif	" "		la-a	my, masc:
				lai-a	" "
				lai-a	" "
				lui-a	" "

GRAMMAR.

Pronoun			Pronoun		
	ta	ny. fem		tas	her. fem:
	tai	" "		tas	" "
	tai	" "		tais	" "
	tan	our, com: gen:		tais	" " "
	tain	" " "		tais	" " "
	tain			tais	" "
	tak	thy, your, masc:		tasn	their, com: gen:
	taik	" " "		tasn	" " "
	taik	" " "		taisn	" " "
	tat	thy, your, fem:		tdisn	" " "
	tat	" " "		taisn	" " "
	tait	" " "		taisn	" " "
	tait	" " "		taisn	" " "
	tait	" " "		taisn	" " "
	tait	" " "		pen	determinative pronouns the, this, masc:
	talin	our, com: gen: plu:		pen	" " "
	talin	" " " "		ten	the, this, fem:
	tailin	" " " "		ten	" " "
	tailin	" " " "		ten	" " "
	taitn	" " " "		apen	these, com: gen:
	taf	his		apu	" " "
	taif	"		apu	" " "
	taif	"		kua	reflective pronouns 1st person
	taif	"		ku-a	" "
				su	3rd person
				tes-a	I myself
				tes-ek	thou thyself

GRAMMAR.

Pronouns				**Adverbs**		
	läs ef	he himself			nen	no, not, negation
	läses	she herself			en	has sometimes the value of a negation
	läse n	they themselves			nent	negation
	ha	with pronoun affixed has the reflective form of "self"			nent	neg: when the verb is plural
	ua neb	everyone, one all.			nen pu	never
	ua neb id				nen seh	no time
	Ki	an other; the antithesis of the above			nen	combined with adjective forms Greek A privative
	Pua	the one			nehau	some few
	Ki Ketta	the other			ben	no, none
	ru	there, the, so, thus			bennu	" "
	nim	who			bennu	" "
	ax	who what; when alone is an affirmative			sen	" "
	lennu	each, how			'bu	" "
	au	a person			bu	" "
	neb	all, every, each			am nen	do not (look on vals)
	nien	a certain man			lem	is used for not
	men	a certain woman			lem	" " " " "
	en	Relative pronouns who, which			ia	yes, affirmative
	ent	" "			ia ax	wherefore, so
	enti	" "			ma	as, like
	a	prefixed to a word has the sense of a rel: pron:			ma	" "
					mati	like, as it were

GRAMMAR.

	Adverbs	
	xer	like, similitude
	hert	up, above
	haru	besides
	haru	"
	haru	"
	put api	at first
	hru neb	daily
	men	"
	emen	"
	sep	a time, with numerals, once, twice, thrice &c
	heh en sep	indefinite number of times
	tata	for ever
	em nehem	again, a second time, renew
	em nehem	"
	em mau	also, anew
	em mat	" "
	em maut	" "
	ma ut tut	likewise
	ma ut tut	" "
	em ter	when, on account
	ha	behind

	Adverbs	
	queb	formed a second time, literally at second hand.
	ker	where (after verb), only
	shaa	&c(?) until, from
		adverbs are formed by prefixing these hieroglyphs to prepositions and nouns, as
	em hnu	besides, in addition to
	em hert	above
	em hert	"
	em tata	for ever
	em xat	before, after, when
	em neser	fortunately
	em ra	indeed, verily
	em hru	besides, in addition to
	em hru	" " "
	en xat	after, near
		affixed to certain preposition form adverbs, as
	er hert	to the above
	er hat	at first, firstly
	er pehui	at the end, lastly
	ensa	behind, after
	er ma	at the place of
	er heh	constantly, for ever
	er tata	for ever

GRAMMAR.

	Adverbs			Prepositions	
	or mad	likewise		ast	then
	or aker	excessively		xeft	when
	srea ur	the greatest, through the whole, altogether, through		ma	where
	er xa	very much		en	to, of, from, by, or
	er lār	entire		en	,, ,, ,, ,, ,,
		form other adverbs by union with prepositions and nouns		en ka	to
				am	in, from, for, as, amid
	en hert	to the above, up		em	,, ,, ,, ,,
				ma	
		,, ,, ,, ,,		er	to, towards, for, to be, from, than
	en tata	for ever		her	so as to, on, of, from, on account
				her·	,, ,, ,, ,, ,,
	her enk	because, above		en her	before
	her enh	same as much as in me··		her ga	on, on top
	xar enk	therefore		xeft	facing
	er enk	that, which, where, inasmuch as, It generally begins sentences and follows the verb, Tut, to say		hat	in
				kar	under, to, course of a day
	ma enk	as if, in the same manner		fina	with, by, and,
				her	and (conjunc:)
	tar enk	when		er her	with, together, towards
	pen enk	where		xer	to, forth,
	pa enk	where		sher	,, ,, ,,
	her nu	so, in the same manner		am	to, in
				am	,, ,,
	embak	before		em tū	before
				em ha	,,
				er ha	,,

GRAMMAR.

		Prepositions, conjunctions				conjunctions, interjections
	Karha	before time		as	lo! behold, then, whilst
	Karpa	behind		ast	" " " "
	em sa	"		astu	" " " "
	em sa	"		ast	" " " "
	em tab	instead		astu	" " " "
	ma	instead of, like, as		ask	" " " "
	er ma	to, besides, then, with		ast	" " " "
	en su	after		tar	after, while, then
	en su	"		xeft	when
	nas	about		an	for, by, of
	an	by, with, from, according to		ax	how much
	an	by		ax tara	what now
	ar	because, to, towards when.		er ax	how much, to how great an extent
	ermen	until, unto		is ax	let it be, therefore
		conjunctions are often omitted		paii	what? how?
	ha	and		xer	for, but,
	her	"		ker	now, but
	her	"		ka	" "
	har	and, (these are of subsequent to Ptolemaic times)		Ki tet	otherwise said
	hna	and		her max¹	but after, but when
	hna	"		Ki tet	otherwise said
	repu	or else, nor, or, either		em	inasmuch as
	em repu	or, nor			Interjections
	mak	for, because		a	Oh!
				a	Oh!

		interjections, verb				Verb
𓏤	a	oh!		𓏤𓏏 〰	au enti	having been
𓏤·	a	oh!		𓏤𓃭-𓃭	au liu	" "
𓏤𓀁	a	Oh!		𓏏𓃭	au lû	" "
𓁹𓏲𓏥	hai	oh!		-𓃭-𓃭	liu liu	it is
𓅓𓀁𓏥·	haii	Oh!		𓆓〰𓃭	ann ef	he is
𓅓𓀁	Ka	Oh!		𓏤 or 𓏤 〰	placed between the root and the nominative case forms the imperfect
𓅓·	Ka	Oh!			

		Verb "to be"		〰𓏤𓆓𓏏	an au her	I was, I was about
𓊪𓈖𓈖	an	is		〰𓏤𓆓	an au her	" " " "
𓊪𓃀	pu	it is		𓆓〰𓏤𓆓𓀀	an an ut ⎱ are passive forms of
𓊪𓃀	pu	" "		〰𓏤𓃀𓃭	an au ut ⎰ preceeding one
𓏤𓏺	ar	is, (frequently precedes pu; ar is often placed at commencement of sentences)		〰𓏤	the Verb is connected with its subject, either immediately or through the particle "n" or "an"
𓏤𓏤𓏺𓏤	aru	plural conju: of "to be"			
𓏤𓏲	au	to be; to exist. is			
𓃀〰𓏤𓏲	mau	signifies similitude of condition			
𓏤𓏲𓀀	du-a	I am, I was			
𓏤𓏲—	au-k	Thou art, thou wast, masc			
𓏤𓏲𓍯	aut	thou wert; thou wast, fem			
𓏤𓏲𓅓or𓀀	auf	he is, he was			
𓏤𓏲𓂋or—	aus	she is, she was			
𓏤𓏲〰𓏤	au nu	we are, we were			
𓏤𓏲𓏤〰𓏤	auten	ye are, ye were			
𓏤𓏲𓂋〰	ausen or	they are, they were			
𓏤𓏲— 〰	ausen or	" " " "			
𓏤𓏲·〰	ausen	" " " "			

Index to geographical names.

GEOGRAPHIC.

	(Asairi) neb Amenti	(Osiris) Lord of Amenti		sulēn tai	King of the two regions
			1		16
	Abt	Abydos 2		meh-ra	S. E.
	Sas	Sais 3		resh-la	U. E.
		4		debet-ta	Land of the Crocodile (God)
	Jattu	Ethiopia 5		meht	E. E.
	Nub	Ombos 6		resh	U. E.
	Shenu	Senek 7		sulēn res	King U. E.
	Noant	Mandos 8		sulēn m	„ „
	Ab	Thebes 9		sulēn res	„ „
	meht	Egypt 10		anefu	Upper country 25
	resh	Egypt 11			Lower country 26
	resh, nu resh	Egypt land of the South 12			Upper Egypt / Lower Egypt 27
	meht nu meht	Egypt land of the North 13		Xamu	Egyptians 28
	resh	Egypt 14		Xamu	„ 29
	meht	Egypt 15		Xamu	„ 30
				Gama	„ 31

GEOGRAPHIC.

	Transliteration	People of Up. & L. Egypt			Transliteration	Egypt	
		Egypt 32			Xanv	Egypt	s/eon?
	Xamu nasi	Egyptians 33			Kamu	Egypt	
	Xamu	" 34			Xamu	Egypt	
	Xamu	" 35				"	
	Xamu	" 36				"	
	Xamu	Egypt 37				Up. Egypt, land of winged sun	
	Xamu	Egypts				Up. Egypt	
	Xamu	"				Egypt	
	Xamu	"				"	
	Xamu	"				"	
	Xam	Egypt				Up. Egypt, land of r̃ʃ	
	Xamu	Egypts				L. Egypt	
	Xamu	Egypt				L. Egypt	
	Xamenai	the two Egypts				" "	
	Xam	Egypt				" "	
	Xami	the two Egypts				" "	
						" "	

GEOGRAPHIC.

Symbol		Name	Meaning	No.
		S. Egypt		37 cont.
	Ra en res Thebes			38
		Thebes		
	Abt	Thebes		
	Abt	Thebes		
	Abt	Thebes		
	Abt	Thebes		
	Kars em abt	Necropolis of Thebes		
		Thebes		
		Thebes		
	Abt	Thebes		
	Abshek	Thebes		
	am	Thebes "the graceful"		
		Thebans		
	Apt	sanctuary of Thebes		
	Apt	Thebes		
	Apt	Thebes		
	Apt	Thebes		
		Thebes Sanctuaries		
	Shu, Ma	Thebes the city of (Truth) Amen.		
	Meroe	Upper Egypt		39
		Kalabshe city		40
		Samneh city		41
		Laldpolis city		42
		Hermonthis city		43
		Coptos city		44
		Dendera city		45
		Abydos city		46
		Abydos city		47
		Abydos		48
		Ombos city		49
		Lycopolis		50
		Aphroditopolis		51
		Speos city, or maybe Artemideos		52

GEOGRAPHIC.

Hieroglyph	Name	Location	No.	Hieroglyph	Name	Location	No.
	cynopolis	cynopolis	53			Memphis	
	Menfer	Memphis	54			.	
	Sas	Sais	55			.	
	Sas	Sais	56			.	
	Xoum	Xoum	57			.	
		Heliopolis	58			Memphis, the City of Pthah	
		Mo Memphis	59			Memphis	
		Phile	60		senem	Syene	66
		Abo city	61			Latopolis	67
		Athritis	62		Aaru	Aturluchis	68
		some part of Egypt	63		Aaru	Arlaluchis	69
		" " "	64		Hanes	Hanes Japhanes Daphnæ	70
	Menfer	Memphis	65			Hanes Jahpenes	71
	Menof	Memphis			Henaat	Hanes, Jahpenes	72
	Menefer	Memphis			Henaat	Hanes, Jahpenes, a city of Neith	73
						El Siout	74
					Anu	Heliopolis	75

GEOGRAPHIC.

	Name	Place	No.		Name	Place	No.
	San	Janis	76			Ethiophia	85
	Jannt	Jentyra, Dendera	77			Ethiopia	
					Jat	Ethiopia	
	sebak	Crocodilopolis	78		Jut	Ethiopia	
		Jentyra, Denderah	79			"	
	Sesau	Sais city	80			"	
	Sas	" "				a city of Ethiopia taken by Amunoph III.	
	Sas	" "				Ethiopia	
	Sae	Sais				Ethiopia	
	shenti Sais	Living in Sais, or Ruler of Sais				A Southern City taken by Amunoph III.	86
		Hermopolis or Oshmoonayn	81			a city in which Thoth was worshipped	87
		" "			Baru	Philæ	88
		Sine city	82		Rebu	Arabia	89
	Pant	Arabia	83		Rebu	Arabia	
	anxem		84				
	Jut	Ethiopia	85				

GEOGRAPHIC.

Hieroglyph	Transliteration	Meaning	No.	Hieroglyph	Transliteration	Meaning	No.
	Ashuar	a part of Arabia	89		Rulénef	Lydian	
	Serhar	may be Scythians, whom Pliny calls Attacori or Joccari	90		Sert	Syria	95
	Jukeri	Joccari, Scythians	91		Ser	"	
		a people living south of Egypt, conquered by Rameses III	92		Seruf	"	
	Nahsi	Negroland	93		Babru	Babylon	96
	Nehsu	Negroes			Shairulan	arab. probably the origin of Saracen	97
	Jurusu	Negroland			Haru	Arab	
	Jaruua	"			Haru	"	
	Hesh	"			Sharmau	Some part of Arabia conquered by the Egyptians	
	Xas	"			Sharman	"	
	Rulennu	Lydia	94		Smehu	one of four races which are usually named together	98
	Ruléinu	"			Auker	Auker.	99
	Rut	Lydians			Rumenen	may be Lebanon, A land conquered by Rameses III	100

GEOGRAPHIC.

GEOGRAPHIC.

	Name	Description	No.		Name	Description	No.
	Shaak	a nation conquered by the Egyptians	101		Abt	East, Thebes	119
	Henuu	a people in the neighborhood of Egypt, perhaps ONO mercenaries	102		Matau	West country	120
	Abshak	Aboosimbel	103		Karui	Chloe	121
	Arunt	River Orontes	104		Keblu	Coptos	122
	Assuru	Assyrians	105		Katesh	Kadesh, Gadytis	123
	Abu	Elephantina	106		Naharina	Mesopotamia	124
	Abtu	Abydos	107				
	Aruma	Arama, Elymais	108		Nahai	Egypt	125
	Bubas or Bast	Bubastis	109		Nenii	Ninevah	126
	Behni	a town in Arabia	110			King of Phœnicia	127
	Hunen	Ionia	111		Nethru	Tantour, Dendera	128
	Hebai	Bahbait Isidis Oppidium	112		Neb or Nemshem	Eilethyas	129
	Jakem		113			Tantour, Dendera	130
	Habenben	Sanctuary of Heliopolis	114		Pairak	Philæ	131
	Hut	Edfoo, Appolinopolis	115		Pers	Persia	132
	Jurtana	Jordan River	116		Peserk	Pselsis	133
	Jlah	Judah	117		Purusati	Philistria Palestine Philistine	134
	Kenus	Nubia	118		Rakati	Racotis, Alexandria	135

GEOGRAPHIC.

	Sen	Sené, Latopolis	136		Shasa shas	shepherds	155
	Sesennu	Oshmoun, Hermopolis	137		Aaru	Elysium	156
	Senenu	Begbe	138		Ura nu	Great Waters	157
	San	Assouan, Syene	139		Sut Hapi nu	Nile River	158
	Sa	South City	140				
	Semit	Amenti	141		Bab	Sate	159
	Serma	Salmis	142		Hebeb nu	deep waters	160
	Taru	Tyre	143			Hell, fiery waters	161
	Taiha	Gaha	144		Atru nu	Waters of Athor	162
	Tawin	Egypt	145		Atru nu		
	Tahruma	Rome	146		Amam	Groves	163
	Sesher	the Desert	147		Setu	hills	164
	Tahnu	Tohen	148			boundaries	165
	Temeh	Tameku	149		Tema	a fortress	166
	Tat	This	150		Kanana	Canaan	167
	Xita	Hittites	151				
	Ut	Lycopolis	152				
	Xaru	Syria	153				
	Xemi	Selselis	154				

THE NOMES OF EGYPT.

Nome			Greek name	Chief city			region	Deity
		Touf	Antæopolites		Per Har nub		W.S.	Horus
		Tat	Aphroditopolis		Tebti		W.S.	Hathor
		Amef peh	.		Kes		W.S.	Hathor
		Kat			T		W.S.	Hathor
		Res Har	Apollinopolis magna		Tebt, Safoo		W.S.	Horus
			(Arabia)		Per tat Har		E.S.	Horus, Subt or Sexet
		Ampeh	Arsinoites		Crocodilopolis Sebek neter		E.S.	Sebek
		Kuxam	Athribites		Hatäheri ab (Abousir)		E.S.	Har r Xouit
		Snxent	Bubastites		Per Bast		E.S.	Basht
			Busirites		Per H'siri re		E.S.	
			Cabasites					Horus
		Aa	Coptites		Coptos		W.S	Tum or Khem
		Sku Anub	Cynopolites		H r om het saka (ridger)		S. E	Anubis
		Tam	Diopolites		Abt (Thebes		W.S.	Amon
			Diospolites					
					Xebeh	Elephantine		
					Ab		W.S.	
		Sah nesh	Gynæcopolites Menelaites Racotis?					Amon

NOMES

Nomes			Greek name	Chief City		Region	Deity
		Hek Net	Heliopolites		An or Per Ra	L.E.	Isus-aa-s Bull Mnevis Tum & Ra
		Am Shent	Heracleopolites		Xenensu	W.E.	Har Shafi
		Wabt			Hermonthis An Munt	W.E.	Muntu
		An	Hermopolites		sesun		Thoth
					Henagpolis Taru	L.E.	
			Hypselites		Sha s'hetep	W.E	Num
					Nexeb	W.E.	Num Ra Nexeb
			Leontopolites				
		Xepah	Lelopolites		Latopolis Sen, Esneh		Fasht Mar ur
			(Lybia is part of)				
		Amef Shent	Lycopolites		Uet, Lycopolis	W.E.	Anubis
					Sant, Siout	"	
			Mareotes				
		Xa	Mendesius (part of)		Mendes Per ba neb tat	L.E.	Munt, Mando Bi neb tat
			Menelaites		Canopus	L.E.	Amen, Sebek and Horus in succession
			Ombites, (Omboo, Tokens)		Elephantine Ombos		Xnoum
			Onuphiles		Sext neter	L.E.	Sebek Ra
			Oxyrinchites		Mert, after wards Par matah	W.E.	
						"	
		Xem	Panopolites		Apu	W.E	Xem
			Pharbaetites		Hebes	L.E.	Horus Isis

NOMES

Nomes		Greek name	Chief City		Region	Deity
ua Skent Abt		Phthemphu	Juk and Per Atum		L.E.	Jum and Hathor
Ampeh		Phthencotes	semet Per Wat P'tu en Wat		L.E.	Wati
Xenes		Prosopites	Sexem		L.E.	Horus
Sa Uat		Sailes	Sas		L.E.	Neith
		Sethroites	may have been formed with a portion of the Nome of Xent-abt		L.E.	
Shutei		Jentyrites	Dendera Ja neter		U.E.	Horus and Hathor
		Thinites	Teni		W.E.	Anhur
Set Ka		Xoites	Xeouu		L.E.	Amen

Index to the names of Gods &c.

GODS. ETC.

	Ra	the Sun God, Helios 1		Ra	governing Sun
	Ra			Sri en Ra	suns' eye
	na				
	Ra			Ra	Originator, Life
	ura	Ra with Uræus,			
				Ra	(Horus) Ra
	Ra				
	api Ra			Ra	
	api Ra				
	Ra			Ra	
	axut	Ra on the Horizon, the young Horus		Alu	a solar God, 2
	hut	celestial Ra		Alu	The Solar disk
	Ra	feminine Ra		Alu	
	Ra any	Life giving Ra		Amen	the God of Thebes, the hidden God, the unknown God 3
	Ra			Amen	
				Amen	often the first character of "Amen meri Ramesee.
	Ra				
	Ra ma	Ra Truth		Amen Ra	Amen who is Ra
	Ra any	the Life giving Sun		Amen Ra	
				Men Ra	Amen Ra
	Ra			Amen Ra	

GODS. ETC.

	Ra	first syllable in Rame- ses in many cartou- ches		Nef Knuph	
	Amon	Ammon 4			originally used to represent Nef, latterly as letter B
	Amen	"		Nefu	Nef ra
	Amen	"		Nef	" . .
	Amen	"		Hfi	" . .
	Amen	"		Hfi	" . . .
	Amen	"		Amen Nef	" . .
	Amen	"		Net Khem	Neith, Minerva 6
	Amen	"		Net	Neith
	Amen	"		Net	"
	Amen	"		Net Ast	Neith and Sais
	Amen	"		Net	Neith
	Amen	"		Net	Neith queen of the East Divine mother, Lady of Sais
	Aten Ra	Sun's disk, the Lord Ra		Net	Neith
	Aben Ra	"		Net	Neith, masculine
	Uben Ra	Light of the Sun		Net	Neith, Goddess of L. Egypt
	Auben Ra	" " " .		Net	Neith
				Net	"
	Nef Chnubis Xnuph	Jupiter Ammon chnubis of Elephantina chnoumis, Kneph 6		Nu Nu	Abyssus. Mother of Gods, Queen of heaven (is not Net)

GODS, ETC.

Hieroglyph	Name	Meaning	Hieroglyph	Name	Meaning
	Neith	Neith		Sebak	God of Ethiopia probably Seb. Many Kings of Ethiopia were named Sebak helap. Crocodile god
	Net	"		Sebak	
	her neter	ha. a title of Neith "over the temple"		sebak	
	Xons	Khons, Chons, one of the Trinity with Ammon and Maut. Xons, Hercules 7		Sebak	
	Xonsu			Sebak Ra	Sebak the Sun god
	Xons	Khons Lunus		Sebak Ra	"
	Xons aa	Great Xons		Sebak	Khem, Jum the Creator, the phallic god. has the left hand concealed; Amsi, Min
	Xons	Xons Lunus		Xem	
	Xons	Xons		Xem	Kheni
	Xonsu	"		Nam	"
	Seb	Saturn, father of the Gods. The seventh day was Seb's, whence the Jews obtained the name Sabbath 8		Amen Ra	mut-ef Amon xem the husband of his mother. The Mnevis, the bull of Heliopolis
	Seb				
	Seb	Saturn			
	Seb	"		Xem	the a has, evidently, a guttural sound
	Seb	"		Xem	Khem
	seb paut	neteru seb and the divine assembly of Gods		Xem	Khem Lord of Janis
	Seb	Seb, feminine		Xem	The bull, the husband
	Seb	Saturn		Ax pet	the bearer of the heavens

	Amon Ra Xem Ka Mut-ef		set	Sois
	Amon sun god creator, the (bull) husband of his mother. A Trinity, or a Unity with the attributes of a trinity		sat	"
			asit	"
	Xem	Khem	asit	"
	Xem aah	Khem-Sunus		
	Mar Xem	Khem-Horus	aset	"
	Xeb	Khem		"
	Amon Xeb	Amen-Khem		"
			mut-neter	Goddess mother
	Aset	Isis	mut-neter	" "
	Aset	"	mut any	Lifegiving mother
	H'set	"		determin. live of Isis
			HeKath	Isis-HetHetHet
	Aset	"	HeKat	" "
	Iset	"	HeKu	" "
	Sat	"	HeK	Wife of Chnumis
	sit	"		
	sat	"	Sexet or Pasht	Lion head Goddess; beloved of Ptah. Goddess of Bubastis; is probably, Nepthys

/2

GODS. ETC.

Pasht	Pasht or Basht, Lady of Bubastis, Lalōna			N'siri	Osiris
Pasht	"			Hsiri	"
Pasht	"			Hsiri	"
H'siri	Osiris	12		Hsiri	"
H'siri	"			H'siri	"
Asir	"			Bennu	
Hsir-neter	Osiris god			H'siri	"
Hsir-suten	Osiris King			Hsiri neb heh	Osiris Lord of eternity
Hsir Ra neter	Osiris Sun God (used since Ptolemies)			Annefer	the good King of Gods 13
Hsiri	Osiris				
Hsiri	"			Seker Hsiri	Sochan Osiris socharis
Hsiri	"			Hsiri-apis	Osiris-apis, Serapis
User	Victorious			Neb Nak	Lord of the great Serpent Nak
User qah	the Victorious dsto			Har	There were three Horus, Horus, son of Isis, Horus, the new Sun, Horus, (scarab) creator
User-u	of Victories			Har	with whip of Osiris 14
				Har se Set	Horus son of Isis
Hsiri	Osiris			Hera (Xepera)	Horus creator
				Her (Xeper)	" "

GODS. ETC.

	(Har)			Har hur	Haroeris
	Xem Xepera (Horus) Khem-Horus the Creator			Har se Hsi	Horus son of Isis
	Ra er Xeper Aroeris			Har	
	Ra eper Sun creator			Neb en mehi Lord of the North (Egypt) Lower Egypt.	
	Ra User Har the Sun Victorius Horus			Net	the defender, the punisher, aveng
				Net	"
	Har em axu Horus of the horizons: Rising & setting suns			Net nofer	the good defender (of his father)
	Amen Ra Har, Amen Ra Horus			Net	the defender (Horus)
	Ra the Sun Horus			Anep	Anubis
	Ra er pahi Sun of the upper & lower worlds, or celestial hemispheres			Anep	"
	axut-i Horus of the two horizons			Anepu	"
	Ra tai-i Sun of the two regions			Anepu	"
	Har Horus with Amen's distinguishing feathers			Apu	Anubis the judge
	Har Horus			Api	" "
	Har Horus, eldest son of Amen			Apter a	Anubis guide of roads
	Har ur Great Horus			"	" " "
	Har se Hsi Horus son of Isis			"	" "
	Har hur Haroeris			Anup	Anubis
	Har hur "			Anup hetep	

15

GODS. ETC.

	Transliteration	Meaning		Transliteration	Meaning
	Anub	Anubis		Nebtha	Nebthys
	Nubti	"		Nebt ha	"
	Nubti	"		Nebt Shent	Nepthys Sister Goddess
	Anub	"			Providence 17
	Anup	Anubis, Judge of Amenti, of the Dead.			The Good Genius. She ' utu'
	Anup	Anubis Lord of Thebes		Jet	Thoth. Mercury, Lord of letters, Thrice Great God, Lord of scribes, Lord of Osh-moonayn.
	Anup	Anubis - first sign of Amenophis's name		Jet	Thoth 19
	Anup	Anubis		Jet	"
		Anubis the Avenging Judge. (a tiger's skin on a pole)		Jeti	"
	Apuara	Guide of the sun's Orbit		Jet	"
	nub	Anubis		Jetfi	"
	heri ef	a title of Anubis, "belonging to the offerings"		Sas	"
	Amu	a title of Anubis "Devourer of the food of the Dead"		Jeti	"
	Nebt lai	Nepthys, Lady of the two regions 16		Jeti	"
	Nebt	Nepthys		Jeti aah	Thoth Lunus
	Nebt ha	Nepthys		Jet Ma	Thoth - Truth
		a trinity of Isis, Osiris and Nepthys		Neb sxai	Lord of writing
		a trinity of Isis, Horus and Nepthys		Athor	Athor, Hathor 20 Venus, Goddess of Love and Beauty. With a cow's head she represents Tsaha mother of Ra

GODS. ETC.

	Name	Meaning		Name	Meaning
	Athor	Athor, Hathor		Mant	Mando, Munt
	Athor	" "		Mant	"
	Ather	" "		Mant Ra	"
	Acheru	" "		Mant Ra	Mandoulis
	Urt	Athor "		Manlu	Mando
	Meq	Goddess with mouse head probably Athor, worshiped at Athribis		Neb Ualà / Neb Uesep	Mando Lord of the Western Nomes
	Ahi	Name of a god who was called the son of Athor; may be Xons who was son of Athor and Amen Ra 21		Hek Uat	Mando Ruler of Thebes
	Ah			Bai	Goddess of the year 25
	Hai	a Goddess 22		Hru neter	God of day 26
	Hapi mu	Nilus, Apis & nu water 23		Ptah	Ptah, God of Memphis; Vulcan 27
	Hapi mu	Nilus		Ptah	Ptah
	Hap mu	"		Ptah	"
				Ptah	Ptah Pigmy, Vulcan
	Hap mu	"		Suten er	Menofre, King of Memphis
	Hapi mi	Nilus concealer of waters		Suten er	Menofre neb, Ptah King of all Memphis
	Ment	Mando, Munt 24		Suten er	Menofre Ptah King of Memphis
	Ment	"		Ptah lu	Suteni Ethiopian form of Ptah the King
	Ment Ra	Mando Sun God		Ptah	Ptah Hephaistos

GODS, ETC.

	Ptah	Pthah		A. Hsiri	Serapis (a' isprobably an abbreviation of Apis
	Ptah	"		Amhetep	Amothetep 30
	Ptah khan	Pthah the Chief		Imhetep	Imothetep
	Ptah	Pthah		Amhetep	Amothetep
	Sekeri	Socharis a title of Osiris, from the hill of Sokara where he was worshiped		Amhetep	Amothetep, called a daughter of Ra
	Seker	socharis 28		Amset	First Genius of Amenti, one of the four Gods of the Dead He made the mummy case. human headed God. 31
	Ptah Seker Hsiri	Pthah-Socharis-Osiris		Amset	
	Seker H'siri	Socharis Osiris		Ipi	One of the four Gods of the Dead. with a Jackals head. 32
	Ptah han Hsiri	Pthah the Majesty Osiris		Hepi	Second minor God of the Dead 33
	seker	Socharis		Semulef	Third minor God of The Dead; He swathed the body. With a Jackals head 34
	Seker	"		sultef	The same. the cutter of the body.
	Hpi	Apis the bull the crux ansata distinguishes it from Apis the God		snuf	Fourth minor God of the Dead. 35
	Hpi	Apis 29		snuf shealtu ef	
	Shapi	"		Serk	Isis, probably, in one of her characters serk, selk, selchis. 36
	Hepi	"		Serk	" "
	Hepi	"		Serk	" "
	Hepi Hsiri	Osiris-apis or Serapis			
	Hepi Apis	Osirisapis or Serapis			
	Hsiri Hepi Neter nas	Serapis the Chief God			

GODS. ETC.

	Mer	Goddess Meroe. Upper Egypt was called Meroe.	37
	Tape	Goddess of the City, i.e. Thebes	38
	Tafen	Goddess of the City "Tanea" "Tapehanes" Daphne	39
	Neheme	Goddess.	40
	Ament	The nether world, the abode of the Dead. Hades, Hell; The goddess Amenti	41
	Amunt	Hades the Southern semicircle of the Suns apparent course.	
	Anunta	Hades	
	Amenti	Goddess Amenta	
	Ament	Hades	
	Ament	land of Amenti	
	Neb Ament	Lord of Amenti, Osiris	
	Neb Ament	" "	
	Apt Amenti	a name given to three Goddesses.	
	skent Amenti	Dwelling of Amenti	
	Skent Amenta	" "	
	Mekes	a leopard head God.	42

	Mau	Truth, son of Neith	43
	Mau	Truth, son of Horus. Ra	
	Ma	Goddess Truth	
	Maa	" "	
	Ma	" "	
	Ioh	a goddess with a cows head	44
	Aht	Ioh	
	Aht	Ioh	
	At suter	Ioh	
	sot	Ioh, (hearkening God)	
	Mes Ra ta neb.	Born of Ra, lord of earth. (Cerberus) the Hippotamus before Osiris	45
	Sheput	Typhon, the god or god-dess of evil, Hermaphrodite Boars head and foot.	46
	Urt	Immortal applied to Gods Goddesses and Kings	47
	urt neteru	immortal gods as opposed to deified mortals	
	urt neteru	immortal gods	
	urt neteru	" "	
	anx sbau	living stars, living Gods	
		Demon, Liar	48
	app Nak	Apophis the Great Swallower	49

GODS, ETC.

	Nu pet	Horus the dew of heaven 50		Mau	Light God 64
	Atat	51		Nefer Atum	the Good Atum 65
	Ahi	son of Athor 52		Atum	Atmu 66
		53			ape-head god 67
	Ahi	an assistant priestess 54		Hapi	Hapi 68
	Athor	Hathor, Athor 55		Num	Lord of Satin, Num 69
	Ma	Goddess of Truth 56		Num suten xenn	Num lord of some part of Abyssinia 70
	User Ma	Victorious Truth 57		Num Ra	Num sun-god 71
	Mut	Bull 58		Num Ra	... 72
	Xu	Ruling Goddess 59		Set	Set, the Ruler, devil or god 73
	Apt	Hippopotamus Goddess with head of human hair 60		Xeper	Creator 74
	P'neb ta	the Lord of the earth, Horus 61		Athor	Venus, Hathor 75
	Iri en Har	the eye of Horus 62		Ma	Truth 76
	Xeper	God Creator 63		Anka	Anucis 77
				Nu pet	firmament goddess
				Jalann	Chief Goddess
				Pti	Phut, Lybia personified
				Mut	Mouth

Alher	Ather, Hathor, Venus	81
Sti	Satis, Juno	83
Menhi	Menhi great Lady of Xenta	84
Ura	Goddess Uræus	85
Ma	Truth, masculine	86
User Ma	Victorious Truth	87
Mati	The two Truths	88
Num	Num or Supi, the Creator	89
Hapi	Apis	90
Paka	Bull of Socharis	91
Num Ra	Num, sun god	92
Artef em meri ef	Aurora	93
Xoper em shai	Creator of the two fields	94
Xu	Steersman of the Sun's barge	95
Her neteru	Over the Gods, chief of the gods	96
Atef neteru	Father of the Gods Osiris & Ptah are often so called.	97

Nuh	Serpent of wickedness eternal	98
Anxtu	a good serpent, fem	99
Nebt neteru	Mistress of the Gods	100
Meken Mehent	The name of the serpent forming the canopy over the boat of Ra a Goddess	101
Nuh	The serpent of wickedness, borne by nine men who have conquered it; eternal	102
aah(x)tamef	Monthly Guardian	103
Api-am u	Avenging Judge	104
Set	Typhon	105
Set	"	
Pext	Goddess Pext	106
Bar	Baal	107
Jahur	Shoueris	108
Munt Ra	Gryphon with hawk head	109
Ba	the Soul	110
Sebek	suchis	111
Sebek-Ra	Suchis Helios	112

		Heavenly Goddess 113		Ptah	Ptah as stability 123
	Net	Neith goddess of L.E. 114			
	Sevennu	Goddess of U.E. 115		Ka	Frog head father of the fathers of the Gods; a form of Ptah
	Rannu	Mistress of the supplies of the Gods. 116			
	Ji	fire breathing serpent of Hades 117		Pasht Basht	forms of the name of Pasht or Basht Soldia. 124
	Xu	Ruling God 118			
	Nelär Atef	Divine father 119			
	Bas	Bacchus, God of jollity, also of death 120		Mut Uati	Mother of the life Uvei
	Safex or Saf	Goddess of Knowledge Special Goddess of libraries. a fem. Thoth 121		Net	Neith 125
	Sati	Satis 122		Nebt ur mut nelär nav, Neith, great mother of Gods all.	
	Sati	"		Net	Neith
	Sati	"		Ra	the life giving, power-giving Sun, Creating Sun 126
	Sati aa	neb pet, Satis great Mistress of heaven		Har em axu	Harmachis
	Sati	Satis, Great Goddess		Nubt	Nubti 127
	sebt	Sothis Great Goddess			

GODS, ETC.

	Nubti neb ta	Nubti Lord of the earth	127	Urhek	Herald, a form of Isis 134
	Apap	Apophis 128		Seneb	Seneb of Silethya 135 Giver of life & health
	Apap	Apophis speared by Horus		Uati or Seneb	The Genius of the two regions 136
	Shu se Ra	Shu Son of Ra 129 Hercules		Uati	The Genius of L.E.
	Ramni neter	Shu, the named God minister		Seneb or Nishem	Lady of Silethya
	Pa neb tai	The Lord of the two regions, Horus 130		Seneb or Nishem	" "
	Sa sent nefer	Sa the good sister, Napthys 131		Uat	Lady of Heaven
	Nefer Atum	The good Tum 132		Uati	Lady of Tehepre
	Nefer Atum	The good Tum Protector of the two regions		Haphap	Nilus 137
	Nefer Atum xu tai	Good Atum Ruler of the two regions		Renpi or Rpi	The year 138
				Heh	snake head Goddess Creator of visible beings 139
	Meru neb Abt	Meru Lord of Thebes 133		Nebt hetep	The Lady of Peace 140

	Wnnu	the hour 141		Ahi ur	great Ahi, son of the sun 152
	Amset	The four Genii of the lower regions, they had charge of -- The stomach and large intestines 142		Ax pet er	The supporter of the heavens 153
	Hapi	the small intestines		Nebt anx	The Mistress of Life 154
	Tuatmutef	the lungs & heart			
	Kabhsenuf	liver and gall bladder. were placed in vases called "canopus" made in the shape of these deities			
	Supt	Sapti, Sueht, Sothis, Dog star 143			
	Ket	Mistress of Heaven, stands on a dog 144			
	Ranpu	Mars 145			
	Anta	Mistress of Heaven, Regent of Gods, Protectress, life established behind her 146			
	Menk	Lady of the vases 147			
	Sat	satis 148			
	Talunn	Chief of Gods, resident in Hennus 149			
	Rebuu	Pupil of the Sun's eye over the great place" 150			
	Seb aa	neter "Heir of the Gods maker of men" The Great Seb, Saturn 151			

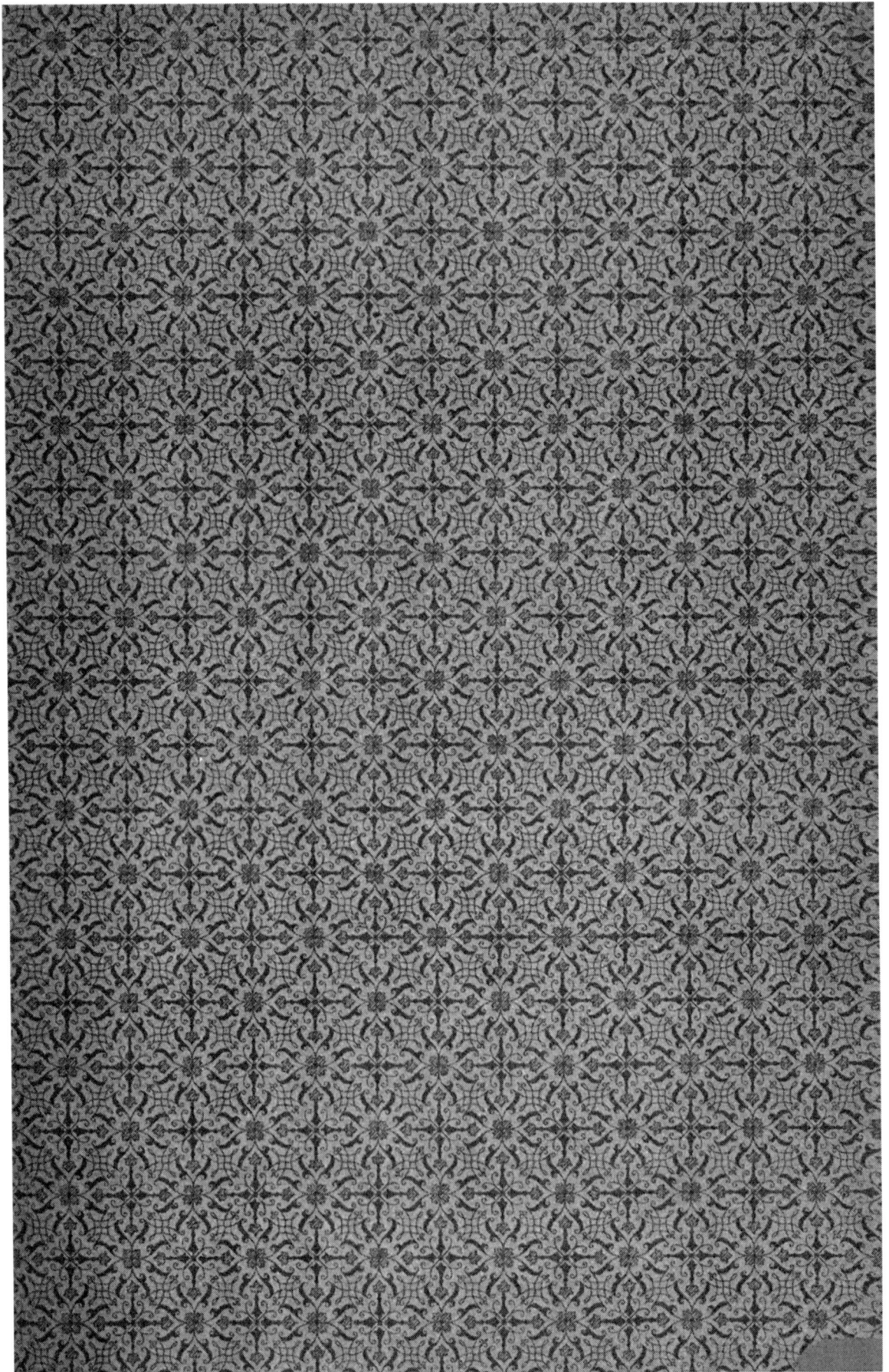

Lightning Source UK Ltd.
Milton Keynes UK
UKOW010950160512

192644UK00007B/4/P